The *Unveiling* of A **MASK**

by Kayl Renee' May

The Unveiling of A Mask

Published 2017 by Leading Through Living Community LLC

Copyright 2016 by Kayl Renee' May

Hardback:
ISBN-10: 0-9983482-6-0
ISBN-13: 978-0-9983482-6-1

Paperback:
ISBN-10: 0-9983482-7-9
ISBN-13: 978-0-9983482-7-8

Edited by Denise L. Majette and Patience C. Mitchell

All Rights Reserved. No part or portion of this publication may be reproduced, stored in a retrieval system, or transmitted in any form or by any means - electronic, mechanical, photocopying, recording, or otherwise - without the express written consent of the author.

For information:
Leading Through Living Community LLC
6790 W. Broad Street Suite 300
Douglasville, GA 30134

DEDICATION

This book is dedicated to our sons, Paul Anthony May, Jr. and Kendrick Antiwon May, whom we love dearly. Thank you for allowing us to be your parents because it has been the most rewarding opportunity. At times, it seemed the toughest responsibility a parent could ever have. We did not know how much love both of you would bring into our lives and for that we are thankful and eternally grateful. There are no perfect parents, but we did what we thought was best with guidance from the Lord. Our prayer is for both of you to become strong, healthy, and productive men in our society. Always keep God first in your life.

Always Remember with God, All Things Are Possible!

PREFACE

Mental illness is real. Schizophrenia is a mental disorder that makes it hard to tell the difference between what is real and what is not, think clearly, have normal emotional responses, and act normally in social situations.

For years, my two sons and I have coexisted with my husband battling this disease, without anyone ever having an inkling of his suffering. Throughout those years I made many excuses to explain why certain things were happening. I even made excuses to myself that I chose to believe to satisfy my own cataclysmic existence. All of my friends and family regard me as strong and valiant, and I am. If only they knew what my mask was really hiding....

We have struggled with this disease since 1998, and it has impacted our lives more than anyone could ever imagine. I feel as though I have been wearing a mask for most of my adult life. No one knows the real me. I don't even think I know who the real me is anymore. I have worn this mask to protect my family through the years, only trusting a few people with the secret I held tight while I struggled in silence.

In this book, you will see just how mental illness can affect the lives of the ones you love the most.

CHAPTER 1

It was New Year's Eve in the country town of Mobile, Alabama. My mother and her sisters decided to attend a New Year's celebration, leaving my cousin and me at my aunt's house without any adult supervision. They decided we were at the age to be trusted, believing we would stay out of trouble.

We were typical teenagers who had already made plans just as soon as they told us of their New Year's plans. Due to the ever-failing trust issues with my mother, this was very new to her. My mother was very strict; she never trusted anyone. Being the strict parent she was, she really didn't trust me.

Acting like the teenagers that we were, we decided to invite my cousin's boyfriend and some of his friends over to bring in the New Year. Even though I was older, I did not have a boyfriend or any suitors in sight. As our guests arrived, a guy whom I had seen at school before arrived with them. He was a little older than my cousin and me. My cousin's boyfriend and the other guys were dancers at our high school and very popular in our little city due to their talent.

I had always known my worth, even as a teenager. It was a very important lesson that was taught to me as a little girl. My lineage consists of very resilient women. Strength and self-worth are qualities they instilled in all of us growing up. Now as I look around me, I see the lack of that in so many preteens and teenagers. They suffer from low self-esteem and not knowing their self-worth.

I wasn't going to give any of those guys a second look because I thought none of them were good enough for me. Their reputations had preceded them and girls wanted to be with them already. I wasn't going to be one of those girls, of course... yet my eyes strayed to one particular guy who I thought was well dressed beyond his years.

During this era, most young men wore jeans and tennis shoes or sweat suits. Paul wore dress slacks, dress shirts, and a brand of shoes called Bostonian. He was very creative with his clothing as well. Though he was the baby boy in the family, he really paid attention to what he wore, as his mother was a seamstress. He would often alter his clothes, dying them and changing their shape. You would have never known that he designed his clothing himself. Once he created his design, he would iron his clothing so well, he had most people thinking that he put all of his clothing in the cleaners. The crease in his shirts and pants could cut you. Whatever cologne he was wearing was the best I had ever smelled (I found out later it was Polo by Ralph Lauren). It made me melt with every breath I took.

Trying to keep a straight face, I had hoped he could not see that I loved the cologne he was wearing, the outfit he was wearing, and the smile he was wearing. All of it was actually wearing me down. I felt as though I was actually melting on the inside. As we sat down to play cards, I could not help but notice that this same guy had the prettiest teeth I had ever seen. They were snow white with one little gold tooth on the side, highlighted by his chocolate skin tone, and glistering brown eyes highlighted by the chandelier. He had the biggest smile ever.

I could hardly play cards for paying attention to his smile, which my cousin and the other guys seemed to notice all too well. He was also the one with the car, which was another plus. Most guys his age and in our school were still walking or catching the bus.

I really didn't say too much to him or anyone else that night, not wanting to give away the fact that I was definitely interested in this guy. After the card game, he left and my cousin's boyfriend stayed behind. I thought this was the perfect opportunity to find out a little more about this guy other than whether he could dance. I asked the same question the rest of the night: "Are those his real teeth?" They just couldn't be because they were just too pretty.

They asked if I was interested in him, and of course I lied and answered, "NO!" When he returned to pick up my cousin's boyfriend, on the ride home, he told him of my many questions about him. They told him that I was in fact interested in him.

The next day, he paid a visit to my aunt's house and asked for little ole me. I was flattered because I knew of his reputation. He could have any girl he wanted. All the young ladies in our school wanted to be with him because of his dancing abilities, because of the way he dressed, because of the way he smelled, because of how handsome he was, because of how slim fine he was, and because he was just different.

He was there for me. "SCORE!" Flattered, to say the least. I smiled all the way to the door. Luckily, I was dressed real cute, showing my long beautiful legs with my white ruffled shirt, half-jean half-white mini skirt, white tennis shoes, and white ruffled socks, because he was well dressed to the "T" again.

A little overdressed for just a drop-by, I thought. I would find out later that this was a part of his everyday dress. He didn't know the meaning of dressing down. The aroma from his cologne again was drawing me closer in. He was so polite to my family and me during this visit. My aunt just fell in love with him.

He asked me if I would go out with him one day. I agreed, not knowing how my mother was going to react because even though I was able to date, I had never really been out on an official date. I was willing to take the chance that she and my father would say yes. We exchanged numbers and he said, "I like you because you seem different from the rest of the girls I have dated." I thought that was just one of the lines he would tell all of the young ladies he was trying to date.

With my smart mouth, I replied, "I am different and you will be wise to not forget that." Thinking to myself, "Why return with a smart remark?" Remembering what was embedded in my head from family and friends, "I will never keep a man with my smart mouth and bad attitude," I hoped that he was up for the challenge. He just smiled as he walked away.

If only he knew then that I had already fallen in love with him at first sight. Overnight I had already planned our entire life together. The dating timeframe, to his proposal, our wedding, our first home, to our children. I had it all planned without fault. He was going to be my forever husband, no doubt about it.

Paul had a magnetic personality that would draw people into his world. He was always making jokes, keeping everyone around him laughing, always the center of attention everywhere we went, the life of every party he attended.

He would do the craziest things to have fun. One in particular comes to mind. We had a hill in our city that led to a big dip from a grocery store to a busy street. My friends and I would pile into the car with him and allow him to do this run repeatedly. We were teenagers having fun. We didn't even think about how we were putting our lives in danger every time we got into the car to do this because the dip led to a busy street. We could have been killed each time! I didn't care as long as I died with the guy that I had fallen in love with at first sight. It was worth it. Yes, I was crazy in love and everyone could see it.

He was always a fast driver. We would frequent Dairy Queen for an ice cream cone in the evenings after school. After we would leave Dairy Queen eating our ice cream talking and laughing, he would abruptly hit the brakes so that the ice cream cone would smash in my face. We would laugh for over an hour about that. He would kiss and eat most of it off of my face. Yes, that was the cutest and sweetest thing to me. It just made me love him even more.

Though he had this comical side to him, he was also one of the most compassionate young men that I had come to know. He would pull over and offer anyone assistance if he saw they were broken down on the side of the road, trying to change a tire, or anything. Anyone who was asking for donations, food, or had "Will work for" signs, he was going to give them whatever he had. If he saw people in need, his heart just went out to them. If he didn't have anything, he would go and try to borrow it from family and go back and give it to them. This was unseen in young men back in our day. At least I had never seen it.

Even though he was in a dance group called the School Boys, he didn't attend classes often so his mother insisted on him getting a job. His mother always taught him the importance of having his own money, maintaining his personal appearance, and taking care of his family.

He began working for the county of Mobile at County Services in Citronelle, Alabama at the age of 17, which was the reason he had his own car when most guys his age were still walking to get to where they wanted to go. He would win over his co-workers with his witty personality, making it easier to get them to teach him how to do different skills on his jobs, which is how he learned to drive trucks. He understood that he had to make it on his job without having an education. He took his employment very seriously even before he started a family. Always early for his shift, never missing a day, always professionally dressed, and of course, smelling extremely good. I remember the county would wash their employees' uniforms. Most employees complained because the uniforms had a funny smell to them. Not Paul's uniforms because he covered them in cologne every morning before work. You couldn't wash that smell out even if you tried. Yes, he was still wearing his Polo cologne that he was wearing when I first fell in love with him. Yes, it was love at first sight, or you could say, "SMELL!"

We dated for a couple of years. We were always together. If he wasn't at work, he was at my house. One of my chores was to have the house cleaned and dinner cooked by the time my parents arrived home from work. He loved the idea that I knew how to maintain a clean house and how to prepare a meal. His family used to ask him where he had been eating every day, because he would never eat at home anymore.

Yep, I knew the way to his heart was through a meal. Though he had a slim build, Paul always had a hearty appetite.

The other awesome thing about Paul is that he would always offer to buy food for me to cook. He would buy a meal for each of us from McDonald's or Burger King if I didn't have time to cook. This showed that he wasn't just a taker, but he also was a giver. That was definitely a plus in my book.

Things were going well between us until our breakup for a year when we both dated other people. Even though we dated other people, I always knew we would end up back together. I just knew we had real love between us. He needed to see what a catch he had in me because he was still excited about how many girls he could have, like most young men his age. I wasn't going to share him. I was too in love and he was too important to me to share him with anyone else. I would rather be without him.

I remember one instance of Paul's kindness. The guy that I was dating at the time and I were at the bank. The guy's car had broken down. Paul was running errands with his mom and saw us with the hood up. It was so funny because Paul had stopped to help us and his mom was fussing up a storm, but he would not leave without trying to see if he could help or offer us a ride. That was just the type of guy he was. Maybe he was trying to show me his heart.

His mom said, "Leave their asses right there." She never minced her words, and of course I wasn't her favorite person at that time because I had broken up with her son. I wasn't her favorite person before that because I was dating her son. That was her baby boy. I don't think anyone would have been good enough to date her beloved son.

I remember when the guy I was dating at the time and I were walking in the area where we lived. Paul was driving past us. Of course he stopped and spoke to us both because that was just the type of guy he was, and because he wanted to see me, and my reaction to seeing him. I guess it worked because after Paul drove off, I remember the guy I was dating said that we needed to break up. He said that every time I saw Paul, he saw stars in my eyes. Knowing he was correct and knowing that I was indeed still madly in love with Paul, we did break up that day. Luckily, the guy and I broke up because I later found out that he had gotten a young lady pregnant. It never bothered me because I never saw him in my future. That spot was still filled with images of Paul as I dreamt.

Everyone could tell that I was still in love with Paul. They could see how much I was missing him, but I had to know that he felt the same way about me—that he was missing me and that his heart was in turmoil like mine. Paul and I did not get back together immediately. By this point he had missed my senior prom and graduation from high school, which he has always regretted, and talks about even now.

Me, High School Graduation 1988

CHAPTER 2

Paul and I had begun to talk on the phone a little more. I had shared with him that I was going to the Keith Sweat Concert with some friends of mine. He was so scared that someone else was going to have me that he called my mom to check on me, he said. He knew it was after my curfew and that I was not at home.

Needless to say, I was put on a two-week punishment. There were no gray areas with my mom. She thought he was the best guy, just looking out for me. Right!

I had captured a towel that Keith Sweat threw into the audience. I would always have that towel with me because I knew it would irate Paul. I guess he thought I was going to go marry Keith Sweat. Could that have been the reason he was so jealous - jealous enough to get me in trouble? He was the only one that could call my mother and check on me. He was fine with that.

After all the longing we could stand, we finally got back together. We dated for another year, blissfully in love. Paul loved going to the movies. A dollar movie theater had just opened up in our town. I think we went to the movies four or five nights a week. Paul had a little yellow standard shift car that wouldn't crank when we were ready to leave the movie. We would sit in the parking lot talking, waiting for nearly everyone to leave (or at least anyone we knew) because we would have to push the car to start it, and then Paul would jump in to drive it. That was the most embarrassing time of my life, and the funniest time as well.

We were having so much fun together and the love was growing deeper and deeper. Finally, we just could not stand being apart anymore. He proposed to me before I went off to basic training for the Air Force Reserve. I told my parents that I was leaving a week before I actually had to report for basic training. We stayed in a hotel in downtown Mobile for the entire week, never leaving the room. We ordered pizza the entire week. We were living off of love alone. It was the most magical moment of my life. After spending so much intimate time together, I wasn't sure if I could actually leave him for 3 months.

We were truly heads over heels in love with one another. The love was so strong; it made this an extremely hard time emotionally for both of us. He would send letters and cards with the sweetest words, and he would wait by the phone for me to call, saying all the right things that a lonely young woman wanted to hear.

When I returned home, everywhere we went people told me how much Paul had missed me, saying how miserable he was with me away. I already had all the letters that my family had written me while I was in basic training and technical school; reminding me how much Paul was missing me and how much time he was spending visiting my family so he could feel close to me. When he wanted to go out at night or to the beach he would have my cousin or one of my close friends to go with him, so no one would say he was being a naughty young man. I thought that was super sweet.

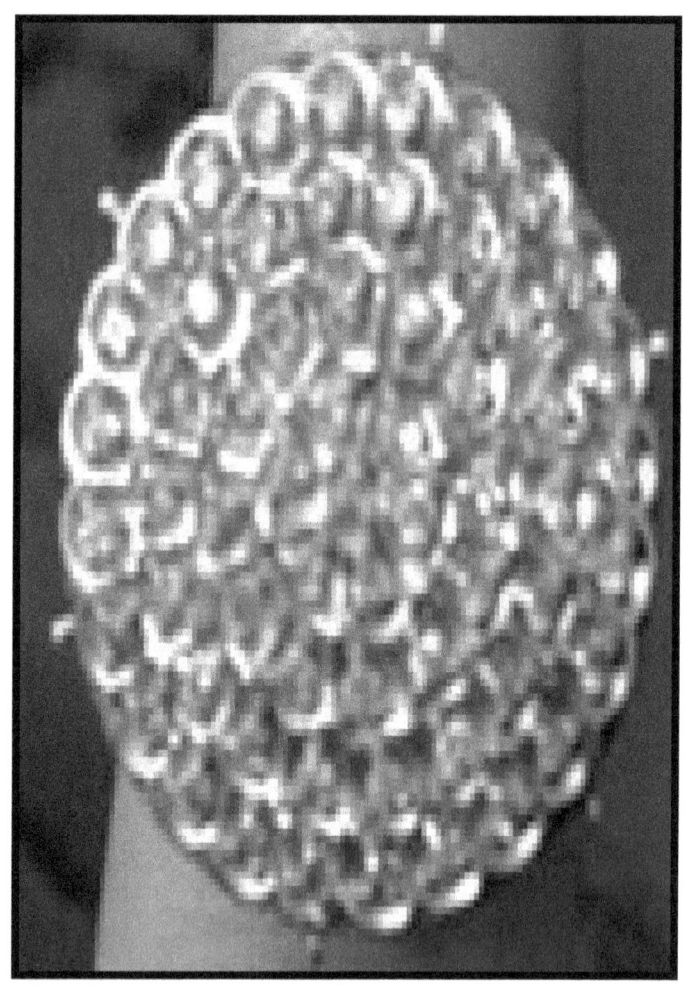

*The Famous Engagement Ring That
Was Given
"Will You Marry Me?"
"YES!!! BABY YESSSS!!!"*

Air Force Reserve 1989

Sending My Love A Smile

Getting Ready to Call My Love

My Love "Always Thinking of Me"

CHAPTER 3

We only had a couple of months to put together our wedding because I absolutely wanted July 29, 1989, to be my wedding date. I really don't know the reason that particular day was so important to me because it did not hold any significant meaning to Paul or me. I worked very hard to make this the best day ever because I was marrying the man I loved more than life itself. I almost drove my mother and aunts crazy because of the time constraint and I wanted things done how I wanted them done. After all, it was my day to marry my man. Oh, how I adored this man. I felt as if I was in Heaven when we were together. He accepted me just as I was, attitude and all. We spent every moment we could together. He treated me like a queen and was such a hard worker. I knew he would be a great provider for his family if we ever decided to have kids. At this time, neither of us really wanted to have children.

On July 29, 1989, that long anticipated moment was here. We were going to be Mr. and Mrs. Paul and Kayl May. I remember having to go and pick up something from my aunt's house and I saw Paul coming towards me with his friend in the car. I was driving my mother's sapphire blue Grand Am. I hit a quick U-turn and sped off. All I could remember was that the groom was not supposed to see the bride the day of the wedding. It all happened so quickly, but I remember laughing so hard until I cried. It was like I was in a wedding day movie. It was completely hilarious.

Finally, I arrived at the church in anticipation of my wedding. The church was decorated in red and white, which were my favorite colors. There we were, standing in church with all our family and friends to share and witness in the moment of two souls becoming one. Seeing the perfect couple uniting before God and all. Our favorite song by Keith Sweat "Make It Last Forever" began to play, and our family and friends began to stand in amazement of the bride beginning to walk down the aisle.

I remember coming down the aisle hearing my youngest aunt on my mother's side say, "I's married now," and laughing. My family knew this was the happiest day of my life. I really wasn't the traditional type, caring about if I had something blue, old, or borrowed. My marriage was going to be perfect because of the love we had for one another. Our love could conquer all. I was a beautiful bride and Paul was such a handsome groom. He actually said, "I do" twice before it was time for him to say it. I was the proudest woman alive. I remember telling the wedding party that this was my wedding and we were going to slow it down a little going down the aisle, because I wanted to have my wedding dress on for as long as I could.

We held our reception in my aunt's nice size front yard, as many receptions and weddings were held in a relative's yard back in the 80s and 90s. We celebrated our union with many family and friends in attendance. Most brides would change into a reception or party dress for the reception, but not me. I wanted to keep on my wedding dress just a little bit longer. I really just wanted to savor that moment, wishing time would stand still for just a moment while I smile and just take it all in. My aunts had fixed all of the reception food and my step-grandmother Minnie had done all of the decorations in the yard for the reception. Everything was so beautiful. They really made sure this was a special day for my new husband and me.

Though I was enjoying my friends and family at the reception, I couldn't wait until my wedding night to finally make love to my HUSBAND. I loved the way that sounded. My HUSBAND! I loved having the title of wife. I was so proud to be called Paul's wife.

We stayed in a hotel in Mobile, Alabama our wedding night and what a night it was. I remember it as though it was yesterday. We made love all night long. I remember saying we will be doing this every day. I felt so connected to him as he gently made love to me. How he held me and caressed my body. How he kissed me for such long periods before we began to have intercourse. The way he would look into my eyes when he began to make love to me. He made it so that it wasn't just a physical act. It was like our souls intertwined with one another. The way I exhaled after we were done making love, leaving me longing for the next time. The way he didn't just fall asleep, but rather he held me and rubbed my body ever so softly, allowing those feelings of love to flow along with the blood in my body from one organ to the other. I loved connecting with him, and that has never changed in 30-plus years.

We arose early that morning, hitting Interstate 65 North to spend the rest of our honeymoon in Atlanta, Georgia. For the entire six-hour road trip, we talked, kissed, and reminisced about our dating days as if they were years ago. We were so happy, and everywhere we stopped everyone knew how happy we were, and that we had just gotten married. Of course, we told them the minute a conversation started up, but I'm sure they could tell from all the public display of affection we had going on. Young love, what can I say.

After returning from our honeymoon, we began our lives as husband and wife. I always knew I wanted to make a career out of the military. I had been in JROTC since I was in middle school. Though I fought against all structure of discipline, I truly loved what the military offered. Maybe I just loved that I would be traveling all over the world and could create my own rules? Maybe it was because I felt I loved my country so much that I wanted to protect the freedom that we all had in this great America? Whatever the reason, I wanted to be in the military. I was out of town a lot because I was a reservist on active duty in Mississippi. Being so in love, I did not want to spend my time away overnight. Even though room and board was covered, I traveled home most nights to be with my husband. I could not bear being away from him. I believe if I could have gotten a job with him, I would have at that time. Looking back on it, that would have been hilarious.

We both spoke about having children and agreed that we only wanted one child if I couldn't have twins. Paul had twin sisters so there was a chance that I could become pregnant with twins, which would have been rare. We were pregnant within six months of being married. I remember having traveled to Marietta, Georgia, for two weeks for reserve duty. Of course, Paul drove me, spending the weekend with me before having to leave to report to work that Monday morning. I got so sick overnight and had to leave to go back home. I don't know if I was love sick from missing my husband or sick because of the pregnancy, but it continued throughout the entire pregnancy. I actually was back in Mobile before Paul got off work on Monday. We have laughed about this so much over the years. It felt like I had beaten him back to Mobile.

Though the love was definitely there between us, getting pregnant so early in our marriage, before we had time to get to know one another and while we were still learning to live as one even though we were two separate unique personalities, really put a strain on the marriage. I think all of the responsibilities came a little too fast for both of us to comprehend.

Our first home together was an apartment after we got married. I began to have difficulties with my pregnancy. I was not able to climb up and down the stairs. We dealt with our situation of getting pregnant and the difficulties of the pregnancy by moving out of our apartment, breaking our one-year lease at six months.

We were visiting his brother one day and stopped to speak to an elderly couple tending to the flowers in their yard to tell them how beautiful their yard was. The couple took a liking to us immediately. They let us know that they were thinking about moving to a smaller house or retirement home. They weren't really sad about it; rather, they were reminiscing because they had lived their entire married lives in that house. They would call Paul and me to come over to have dinner with them for the next few weeks. Then they said that they wanted us to purchase their home and make it our home to start our new family. They always said we reminded them of how in love they were when they first got married and started their family. They wanted us to make our wonderful memories in their house.

We purchased that house, moving up the street from Paul's brother, his wife, and their two children. It was a very nice neighborhood, especially for a young couple like us, in our early twenties. It was a little far from the rest of our family, but that was the house we both wanted. He wouldn't have it any other way. His child was going to come from the hospital to a home with his very own room. That was so important to him.

When we learned that we were having a boy, this made Paul very happy. He immediately wanted him to be a Junior, which I didn't have a problem with. After all, Paul was a very good man with so many great qualities. Who wouldn't want their child to be named after such a great man?!

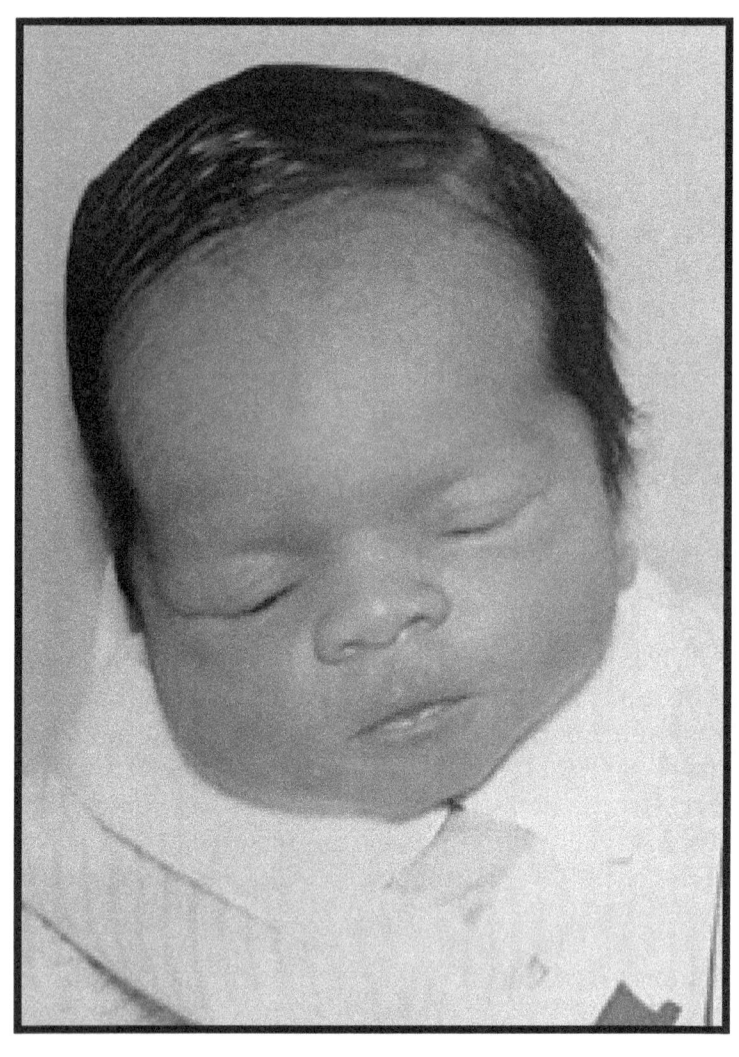

Paul Anthony May, Jr.
October 9, 1990

CHAPTER 4

With our first child, we were still able to travel and have fun enjoying life because that was my parents' first and only grandchild. My mother and father took over. We didn't have a problem with this even though we took our responsibility of being parents very seriously. My parents' attitude allowed us to still enjoy life as young adults as well as enjoy parenthood. We were very appreciative of the assistance.

Those first few years with our only son seemed to go by so fast. I remember us going to church with our son. We were such the perfect little family. Not being overly protective of him, but making sure to protect him from any and all dangers. Some things happened in my childhood that made me very protective of my children. We were as happy as a family as we were as a couple.

We were surprised when we found out I was pregnant with our second child three years later. Our second son was destined to be our child. Paul and I had decided that we were finished having children, so why not make it official? I will never forget that day. I was at the doctor's office getting the paperwork for my spouse to sign papers giving me permission to have my tubes tied. Remember, my body was not my own. We were considered as one unit so we both had to agree to get my tubes tied.

While in the office, the doctor had to do a routine examination. To my unbelief, during this ROUTINE exam, I was already pregnant. I was so shocked, as though I didn't know how this could have happened. I was so scared to tell my husband because we both wanted to have the tubal ligation. I told my husband with fear in my eyes and voice.

When I say he was overly excited that he was having another child, he was really excited--calling and telling everyone in his family including his close friends. Once we found out we were having another son, he was ecstatic. He was at work passing out cigars with excitement. Can you imagine, he wanted to name this one Paul May, III? Yes, he did.

I knew I wasn't ever going to have a girl because the tubes would be tied before I left the delivery room. I wanted the child to have something like my name, or at least the first letter K. I wasn't instantly happy or excited about having another child. Once I accepted the idea that I was having two children, boys at that, I was very excited.

This pregnancy wasn't as much fun as my first because Paul and I began to have more problems early on. I had morning sickness with both of my sons for what seemed like the entire nine months. What made this one different was that I found out I was pregnant at a just few weeks, so it seemed like the sickness was crazy.

Where I had morning sickness with my first son, I had all day sickness with this pregnancy. I remember having to pull over frequently on the Interstate to vomit. I couldn't stand the smell of anything, including that good-smelling cologne that used to drive me crazy in a good way. Now it was driving me crazy just the opposite.

Kendrick May

Towards the end of this second pregnancy, I suspected Paul of having an affair. I didn't have any proof and in reality, I wasn't looking for any proof. I still wanted to have that perfect little family so much that nothing or no one could have broken us up. We were destined to be together. Our love would help us to conquer all, or so I thought.

You know how once you find out something is true, and you have that hindsight type of vision. It's the vision that makes you say, "How could I have not seen that?" or, "Why didn't I question this or that when I saw this or that?" That hindsight makes you realize that you were not living in reality. You had made up and even lied to yourself about things that you felt, or even saw with your own eyes. Once those eyes are open, you feel like a childish schoolgirl that was being stupid for her boyfriend even though she knew something was going on.

This was way more important than a boyfriend cheating. This was something that could potentially ruin my marriage, my family, even take away my sons' father from living under the same roof with them. I remember questioning my husband only once about cheating on me. Of course, he denied it.

I wasn't the type of wife who was looking for clues to see if my husband was cheating on me. I always thought we had the type of relationship that if he didn't want me, he would leave me. We had talked about such things early on in our dating. I always said, "I love you enough to let you go," because to me that's really what love was about. You want to see that person happy whether that person is with you or with someone else. Not saying it wouldn't be hard, but it would be done. I would never want to be with anyone who did not want to be with me, or was staying with me only because they felt obligated because of children. I wanted someone to truly love me and want to be there for his children and me.

Though I loved Paul with every breath that I breathed,

I also loved myself just as much.

I remember this particular day as if it was yesterday. I was sitting at home with the kids and some of my preteen cousins had come over for the weekend. Paul said he was going off to spend some time with his family. He came home a little earlier than I thought he would.

When I asked what brought him back so soon, he said he remembered that he needed to return some movies we rented for family night. This was during the time when you rented movies for a day or so and had to rewind them or be charged extra (even before the big BLOCKBUSTER takeover).

When he left, I could hear a voice say, "Follow him." I never had that feeling of wanting to follow him before, but I did not ignore the voice. I actually told my cousins to watch the boys and that I would be right back. I followed my husband to the movie rental place that wasn't too far from the house. I really felt a little stupid for following him because when he came out of the video store he was alone.

Though the voice didn't say he was with someone, I felt as though he had dropped someone off before he came home. I just knew he was going to pick them up after he left the house. That was the feeling I felt. So imagine how I felt when he got in the car alone. No one was with him.

I sat in the parking lot beating myself up because I should have trusted my husband. I actually felt like I had betrayed his trust, which was something that I have always thought a relationship must have as a foundation to survive. As I saw him get into the car alone, I actually cried because I did not trust him.

I had noticed he went across the street to get some gas while I was beating myself up. I wanted to go across the street to tell him what I had done.

Right at that moment, I saw a young lady come out of

the gas station and get into the passenger side of his car.

The beating up I was doing to myself, I now wanted to do to him. I could not believe he could do this to me, to his boys, to our family. "How could he?" I remember yelling at the top of my voice as I sped out to cross the busy highway to let him know that I saw him. To let him know that I now knew of his BETRAYAL. To let him know that he had destroyed his perfect little family that we had worked so hard to maintain. To let him know that the life he had with me was over.

We had talked about everything while we were dating. I had promised that I would never divorce him except if he cheated on me. As I saw him trying to speed away with the young lady in the car, that conversation came flooding back to me. Even then I was a woman of my word. I knew right then and there that no matter how much I loved him, and I truly still loved him, that I would divorce him. That day I felt the worst pain of all betrayal. When I think back on that time in my life, I associate that pain with giving birth to a child without pain meds. That's how bad it hurt. It hurt to know that you have been sharing the man that you love with someone else. To know that he has been lying to you and you are now questioning everything he has ever told you. How could this happen to our perfect family? How could this happen to the man that I fell in love with at first sight? How could this happen to me?

Then you go through the stage of, "What did I do to make him want someone else?" I had gained weight after having the babies, so I used that as the reason why he cheated on me.

Thank God for the self-worth that he had given me from birth and the self-esteem I had for myself. That phase of making excuses for him and blaming myself was very brief. I did not allow him to use that as an excuse. I was his beautiful trophy wife on the outside, but he had forgotten all that I was for him and our family on the inside. Remember, we fell in love very young, at the tender ages of 16 and 18 years old. What did we really know about love outside of the books we read? Even so, I was not going to let him use me as an excuse for his problem and betrayal. I needed him not to let his ego come before his family. I had to remind him of the woman he married. To remind him of what he once said, that I was the young lady who was "different from the other girls," and why he "thought I was different."

    I had to stand my ground no matter how much I loved him. I had to remember to love myself more. I always knew I would forgive him and that we would get back together, but first he had to remember who I was and why he loved me so. He had to remember the manner in which I stood out. He had to get to know me as the lady I had grown to be. The only way I could get him to see that was to love him enough to let him go.

Always Know Your Worth!

CHAPTER 5

Remember, I had told Paul years ago that the only way I would divorce him was if he cheated on me. Once I had accepted that he cheated on me, which was not easy, I had to divorce the man that I loved so dearly. The man I adored like no other before. Not like this. My words, my action, my voice had to be heard. He had to see me as the strong woman I was raised to be. He had to know I would not tolerate being mistreated.

I remembered something my mother and my aunts use to always say. "You have to teach people how to treat you and how you expect to be treated." I knew my self-worth and it was time he came to this realization. Divorce was the first step of showing him this. Some people believe divorce is the end of life or a relationship. But I do not. I know that it doesn't have to be. For us, it was the start of our real lives.

We did get a divorce. While going through the divorce, we remained in the same house. This was a very miserable time for both of us. I felt as though he should not be at the house and he thought he should be at the house.

I had put him out and taken his clothes over to the house of the young lady that I saw get into his car. He came back several times, telling me that this was his house and that I could not put him out. He brought the police back with him.

They informed us both of our rights. I could not put him out until the divorce was final and I was awarded the house. I went from hurt to anger quickly.

We argued often. He would leave and go to his mother's house sometimes, but he would always come back. I think he thought that if we stayed together while going through the divorce that I would change my mind. What he had forgotten was that once my mind is made up, there is no changing it. Not even for the love of my life. He should have been listening more closely to all of those conversations we were having when we were dating.

I remember a time getting a knife because he had hit that last nerve. I ended up cutting the tip of his thumb off. At that point, I truly didn't care. I just wanted him to leave. He told me that he would call the police on me if I didn't go to the hospital with him. Yes, of course I went to the hospital with him. I wasn't going to jail for him. He had already caused me enough pain, but I wasn't willing to give up my freedom for him or leave my boys.

We both ended up getting arrested for the first and last time ever while we were going through the divorce process. I was so scared when the police came and ordered me to the ground because I had a knife in my hand. While I was in jail, I remember asking the guard for some eye drops because something had gotten in my eyes. He said, "Ma'am, do you know where you are?"

I just cried and cried. He said, "Those tears should get whatever is in your eyes out." I cried even harder.

I could not believe I was in jail remembering all of the lessons my family had taught me to keep me out of this very place. I would not sit down because I thought that I would get some type of disease. It was like in a movie and only the dirty and unclean people were in jail. Well, I was neither and here I was in jail.

I was so thankful that my girlfriend had witnessed that incident and called my mother, who called my father to bail me out. She refused to come to the jailhouse. Thank God she had sent him, which shocked me.

My mother was very strict and said exactly what she meant. She told us to never go to jail because she was not coming to get us out, but she would always love us.

Honey, I needed to be out of jail. I was willing to chance her loving me again. My friend's boyfriend at the time had a sister who worked in docking at the jail. They were trying to get my paperwork rushed so that I could bond out quickly. I was never so happy to see my little daddy when they released me. He didn't say anything. He just hugged me. He could see that I was terrified and had been crying, as my face was fire red and my eyes were all swollen with tears still running.

Thank God my mom did not come with him because I would have gotten an ear full as soon as they opened the doors to release me. I still had to listen to all of that later because she was waiting at the house for me.

It was a horrible and embarrassing time for both Paul and me. He only wanted me to see that he wanted his family. I only wanted him to see how much I was hurting and needed him to leave. I wasn't changing my mind, so it didn't matter what he would say or do. It wasn't going to work. I wanted a divorce.

I think Paul enjoyed being single again for the first week or so. Remember, we did get married young. I'm sure he thought he could have his old life back for a minute or so, but in life you can never go back. The past is called the past for a reason. He soon started to miss his boys and me.

The repetitive calls started, then the visits started, but I wasn't ready yet. I was still bitter. I still only saw the mistakes he had made. I had to learn who I was as an individual. I no longer had the love of my life to depend on anymore.

Though it was hard, I made it work. I went to therapy to work out some of my issues. Though I knew I had something to do with the marriage going down the drain, I would have never let him use it as an excuse. We both dated others during this time. As the saying goes, what's good for the goose is good for the gander. Well, that wasn't so when the shoe is on the other foot. Neither of us could stand knowing that the other was with someone else.

I remember a time that I had invited someone over to the house for the first time and Paul came by unannounced as he often did, still trying to piss on his spot. (Show ownership.)

Paul had never been a person to get into a physical altercation EVER. The guy was getting ready to leave as Paul pulled up. He was all of 6'6" and very muscular as he was going through the police academy at the time, and Paul is 5'11". Size did not matter to him that day. He had prepared to fight for his family. He knew that he did not want anyone else with me or around his sons.

The guy carried a gun and was going to use it because Paul was threatening him. My heart dropped. Right then, I knew how much I still really cared for Paul because I was more concerned about him getting hurt, not the guy. That was the last time I saw that guy. All I could think about was how Paul could have gotten hurt or shot and there would not have been a way I could have lived with that. What would I have said to his boys who worshipped him that their mother caused their father to get hurt or even killed? I had to contemplate whether it was time to end the punishment that we both were going through. Was it time for us to start over?

As time went on we decided that we wanted to be married to one another again. We both made a commitment to one another and meant every word we said. I trusted him like nothing had ever happened.

When you tell people that you forgive them and that you trust them that is what MUST happen. I would never go back into a relationship without trust. I truly believed that he punished himself enough and realized what he had lost because of his mistake.

A mistake is just that. Learn from it and move on.

That's exactly what we did. Though I do not want to make light of it or make it seem as though it was easy to get to this point because it wasn't. Looking back over our lives, we never questioned if it was worth every bit of it.

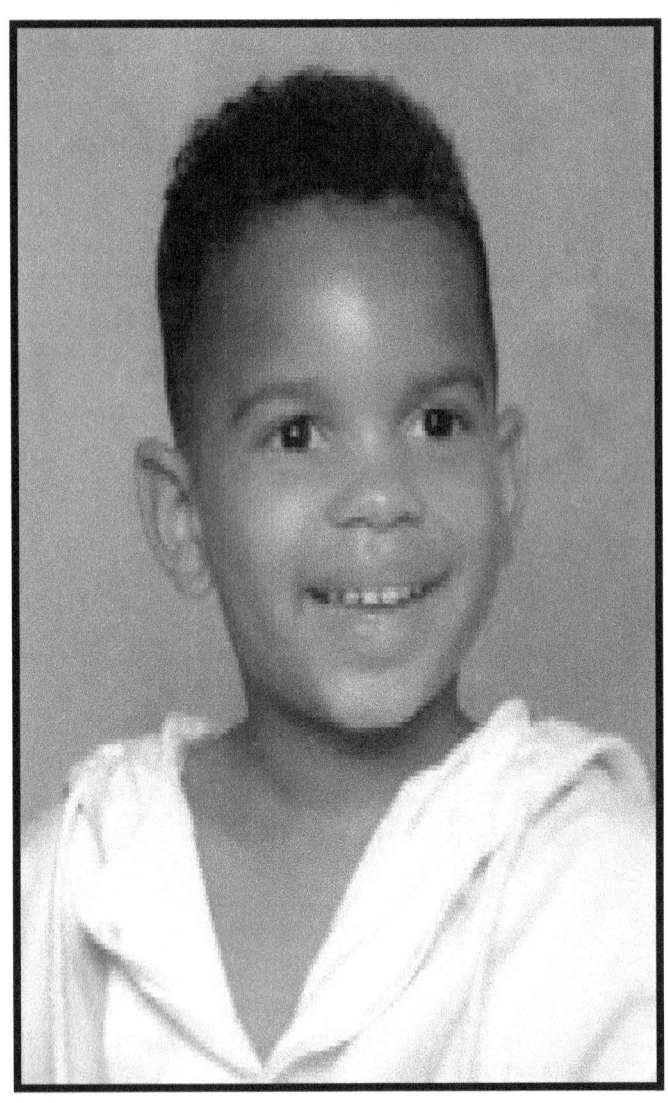

Paul May, Jr.

Kendrick May

Paul May, Jr.

The Unveiling of A Mask

The May Boys

With My Boys

We were so happy being back together as a family. We did everything together. I was completely sure we had done the right thing by getting back together. I thanked God for allowing us a second chance.

The happiness went on for a few years. I thought all the bad things that could happen in our marriage had already happened and were behind us. I knew going forward only happiness awaited us.

Paul and I both came from Christian families. It was mandatory that we were in church and participated in many of the activities of the church as we grew up. It was important to us both that church remained a part of our lives especially once we had remarried.

So it wasn't strange when Paul began to become more involved in the church. We have always known that he had a calling on his life to preach the gospel. He finally decided to accept his calling. Even though I supported him, I did not think he was ready for the task that was going to be put before him. His religion and his family were his top priorities at this time.

I began to notice that he was becoming more withdrawn from his family, from the boys, especially from me. After work, he studied the Bible at every waking moment. I excused the idea, thinking he just wanted to learn as much of the word of God as possible. It wasn't until he began complaining about the way I dressed to attend church that I became concerned. He had this idea that only mothers of the church should wear hats to church.

We both come from a Southern background where wearing suits, ties, and hats when entering the church were considered looking your absolute best. Even though I grew up wearing hats to church because my mom always wore hats, he complained every single Sunday. It wasn't about the religion to me; it was just a style that I picked up from my mother. I also modeled hats at different church functions.

Fashioning hats at church teas as a teenager was very common.

Because he had this idea that only mothers of the church should wear hats and what it meant to be a mother of the church, I wasn't worthy to wear a hat. It seemed as though we were starting arguments out of nowhere, and it was beginning to get out of control. The worst thing is I didn't even know why we were arguing. Looking back in hindsight, this is when he began displaying signs and symptoms of mental illness. He became very demanding that things were done a certain way, which was strange because he never demanded me to do anything. This was particularly upsetting to me because of my strong personality.

Paul began to not want certain people to come to the house anymore. His ruling had demands on even some of our boys' young friends. One particular child was tall for his age and Paul began to look at him as a young man and thought that I might start to have a relationship with him – a boy! I had to stop him from coming over because it would upset Paul every time he came home from work and the little boy was at the house. I could not understand at that time why it upset him so much. I just put it off as Paul being very foolish.

Then he began to complain about one of our next-door neighbors. He said they were picking at him and throwing rocks on the side of the house, but they would only do it when I wasn't there. We had always gotten along with our neighbors, so I didn't know what to think. It sounded so crazy to me, but then why would he make up such a thing? Then again, why would our neighbors that we were friendly with do such a thing?

I did not want to go ask them if they were really doing this. I was afraid of how I might look in their sight. What would I think of a person if someone knocked on my door and asked me, "Are you throwing rocks at the side of our house when I am not at home?" I also knew it would freak them out, thinking, "What is really going on with that person?"

Then Paul began to stay in our younger son's room more after work so that he could be alone. We normally all gathered in the family room after work and activities to spend time together as a family. The family room was the only room in the house with a television because spending time together as a family was extremely important to us both. In our eyes, bedrooms were for sleeping.

We turned our living room into a playroom for the boys instead of having a room looking cute and never really using it. I remember the living room in my mother's house with the furniture covered from top to bottom with plastic. I cannot remember us ever really sitting in or using the living room for anything. Even when my mother would have company, they would either sit at the counter in the kitchen or go to the den.

Paul continued to use our younger son's room for his studies of the Bible after work. He would call me in the room saying they were throwing rocks at the house again, but I could not hear anything or see anyone.

I remember becoming afraid of what may be happening. I didn't have a good relationship with my in-laws at the time, so I really didn't know how to approach them with what I thought was going on with Paul. I knew I needed to let someone know that something was happening even though I had no idea of what was really happening.

I still overlooked the behavior for a while because I was so busy with work, home, and raising two small kids. I finally confided in his brother about the issues that we were having and of course, at first he did not believe me.

Now you have to know and understand about my in-laws. My husband and his twin sister are the babies among the siblings. They definitely played that part to a "T" and the family treated them as though they were still babies. In saying that, his brother could not believe what I was saying because he did not want to believe that his baby brother was having some type of breakdown. He in turn spoke with his sister, so that they could watch him more, and perhaps see some of the symptoms I had told them I was seeing and dealing with.

It's hard to see symptoms sometimes because people who have mental issues get really good at hiding them. They know something is wrong, and they try very hard not to bring any attention to themselves. Everything that they see, hear, and feel seems so real to them. They can see and hear the person that they are talking to or that is talking to them just as if you and I are having a conversation with one another face to face. It's like they are trapped between two worlds.

Paul began to visit his family more, but they would always be very short visits. He would make a lot of excuses that seemed legitimate anytime his family asked him anything, and because he knew his family and I didn't get along, he would use that to excuse why I was saying certain things about him. He was keeping us divided so they would not believe that what I was saying he was doing was actually happening. Divide and conquer, that was his plan.

Paul is a truck driver by trade and he really loved driving those big rigs. He had learned how to drive dump trucks at his first job at 18 years old before they had to have commercial driver's licenses. Once the commercial driver's license was required, he decided to go to school to learn to drive 18-wheelers.

He so enjoyed driving trucks and I was so proud of him because he could drive like no other. I remember other drivers asking him to park their trucks, or whip it around to get into a certain spot. I was always so proud of him because I knew he really enjoyed what he was doing.

It wasn't long that the problems we were having at home spilled over into other areas of his life. He had gotten a job working with an environmental company for residents. He was still doing what he loved doing and getting in more exercise as well, which was what he wanted. He was always afraid he was going to get fat or gain a stomach like he said he saw happen to a lot of truck drivers.

Paul began having problems on his job because he would not answer the radio in the truck when the company would try to contact him. He would actually turn the radio off because he thought they were keeping track of his every move and listening to his every word. He began confronting his coworkers about things he thought they were doing to him. They had no clue as to what was going on or what in the world Paul was talking about.

Although Paul was a hard worker, a great driver, and had a great personality, he was having more and more problems on the job and no one really knew why. They were contacting me telling me of things that he was doing, and I didn't have an answer for them because he was acting the same way at home and I didn't know why. Paul was also working for a friend on the weekends, driving trucks to bring in extra income for the family. They were not complaining as much because they had known him for years and they knew of his comical personality. They thought he was just displaying that side more and more. He was actually a joy for them to be around. Little did they know what was really going on with his mental stability.

Paul always held down a job because he loved to work, drive trucks, and take care of his family. He loved his family and wanted to take care of us, but his mental capacity would not allow him to hold a job for long lengths of time. He was losing his family at the same time he was losing his job because I did not know what else to do.

I could not get him to talk to anyone other than a minister. When he did agree to talk to a minister, if the minister disagreed with anything he said, he never wanted to talk to that minister again. It also made it difficult to persuade him to discuss the situation with anyone else. Most people knew of Paul's family ties in the church, so they always agreed with him that I was the problem because I wasn't in the church as heavily as he was.

It's funny how he could really pull the wool over the eyes of Christians and ministers, even the ones that would say things and say that the Lord had told them to tell us this or that. None of it had anything to do with mental illness.

You have to be so careful when seeking outside counsel. Remember, some Christians can pray for you, but they may not have the background or education to give you the guidance needed. I needed prayer for sure, and definitely believe in the power of prayer.

What I needed as well was for someone to guide me to where I could go and get help for my husband, so that whatever was going on would not destroy my marriage to this man that I loved so much. I needed him and his boys needed him. I needed someone who knew how to help us. I had given up on seeking church therapy because they could not see what I was going through.

At this time Paul was great at making me look as though I was the one with the problem. My lack of patience and tolerance were at an all-time high, and that was working in his favor. Patience had never been a strong suit of mine anyway. Paul would leave and be gone for hours with no one knowing where he was. Friends and family would call and ask was Paul okay because they would see him out and about saying things that did not sound normal.

A lot of people thought that he was on drugs or something like that, because there are a lot of drug users from our hometown. I knew that was not the case with Paul, though. Some things you just know about your spouse and him getting on drugs was one thing that I knew he wasn't about to do.

Others thought as I thought— that something was

going very wrong mentally with him. He was acting out of character, even with always trying to make others laugh or being the center of attention. He always had the funny side that made others laugh.

I continued to pray for God to lead me and let me know what was happening to my family because not so long ago we were extremely happy. I was so confused about it all, yet I couldn't just focus on that because I had two small boys who needed my attention as well.

Taking care of two small ones is hard enough when everything is going well. You can imagine how hard it was for me when I thought at any moment I was going to lose my mind. Trying to figure out what was going wrong with the man that I loved so much and tending to my marriage, which was failing quickly, were emotionally draining.

I finally got his brother and one of his sisters to listen to me and we took Paul to the emergency room. During this time he also had begun to lose weight because he did not trust anyone's cooking. His thinking was that someone was going to poison him or put something in his food to make him lose his mind. Little did he know that was already happening.

He would cook his own food. It wouldn't be something regular, but putting together strange ingredients to make a meal, such as eggs with ketchup, something he didn't usually eat.

When we took him to the emergency room they kept him for three days for observation, as they could see he was having some type of paranormal episodes. At first glance, of course they thought that he had taken some type of drugs. After performing a drug test to rule this out, they knew that it was something else causing it. He was released from the hospital with the instructions to go to the mental health outpatient center. We made the appointment, but he only went to the intake appointment. Neither his family nor I could get him to go back to any other appointments.

I tried to persuade him every way I knew how to go and get some help, but nothing I said or did mattered. He refused to get any help because he refused to recognize that something was actually wrong. It is really hard to get someone with a mental illness to see that something is really wrong with their thinking or actions, because it is all too real for the person that is going through it.

I couldn't take it anymore. At that point, I decided I was going to leave with the children, and leave my husband behind. This was the hardest decision I have ever had to make because I had been in love with this man since I was 16 years of age. I fell in love with Paul at first sight. Even though I had made up my mind, I wasn't sure if I was going to be strong enough to actually do it. I didn't even know where I was going to move. I just knew I had to get away from all of the crazy things that were going on in my life before I lost my mind. I told my parents first that I had decided to move, and of course, they didn't understand and weren't supportive at first. They loved Paul as much as they loved me and didn't want to see our family split up.

They soon saw I was serious. Spending more time at our house and seeing the behavior he was displaying, they then understood and became more supportive.

I told my husband that I was leaving him and wanted a divorce because we were not happy together. I told him I loved him enough to let him go so he could be happy. See, at this point, I blamed myself for everything that was happening because I didn't have an explanation for it. It had to be me because that is what he would tell me. He would say, "It's not me, it's you that is messing up this marriage, our family."

I just know I did not want to be in a relationship so unhappy, no matter how much I loved him and was in love with him. I didn't want my boys to grow up in a home environment with the parents going at it all the time, or the parents barely speaking to one another. Though I loved my husband, I knew I was making the right decision for the family.

One day, I loaded up a U-Haul truck with just enough clothes for my boys and me. I left the house and everything in the house with him. I know some people may not understand this, but material things were not as important as my family happiness. I knew that God had blessed us materially once and he would do it again. Scared or not, I knew I could do all things through Christ.

A strong woman is one who is able to smile in the morning like she was not crying last night.
-Shamia Kegler

CHAPTER 6

When I moved to Georgia, I had nothing but a few clothes for me and the boys. I left my house and all the furniture with my husband. That's when you know you are tired of a situation. I moved here without a job, moving in with my cousin, her son, daughter, and her husband. I had never lived with anyone before, so that was not the best of situations for me, though I was happy to have somewhere for my boys and me to lay our heads and knew we would be safe. We made the best of it. Where else did I have to go, moving there with no job yet?

I lost all contact with my two dearest friends. Looking back, I wonder did I lose contact because I became so busy or because I was embarrassed about what was really going on in my life.

I remember calling one of my good friends from high school because her oldest son was my godson and I loved him like he was my own son. I remember the first year of his life was spent with me. I adored that chubby little boy. I wanted him to know where I had moved to and to have my contact information in case he ever needed me. Knowing I would miss most of his growing up, at least he could contact me if needed.

My job at The Fine Jewelry Store didn't automatically transfer to Georgia. I had to interview all over again and wait for an opening in the department. It took about a month before I was able to start. I was excited about the job, but I was so unhappy being without my husband, the man I had been with all of my adult life. I had been with this man since I was a teenager and I loved him very much. I was very much still in love with him.

When you love someone so deeply, it doesn't disappear overnight, no matter what problems may arise. I know a lot of people will not understand this.

It wasn't long until he began calling me and before you know it, love gave in and he was in Georgia. I did not want him to come stay at my cousin's house because I had not asked her or her husband whether he could stay. Anyway, there were enough of us already in a two-bedroom apartment.

After he arrived, we had to find somewhere for him to stay and I wanted to be with him. I would work all day, come home to get the children fed, bathed, homework completed, and off to bed. While I was taking care of the kids, Paul would visit different churches. He really wanted to be healed and he always had the faith that God would heal him.

People were always drawn to Paul, the humbling spirit about him. They could see something was wrong and always offered him help by talking to him, spending time with him, or giving him money. One gentleman he met at one of the churches actually gave him a car that he was no longer using.

I always felt like Paul was bargaining with the Lord because he wanted to be whole again. He would give everything he had to the church. If he didn't have money to give when he went to church, he would pawn his jewelry to have money to donate. So as much as others were pouring into him, he was pouring back into the church.

After church and after I got the boys together for the night, Paul would come and pick me up. He would go and work at temp agencies while I was at work. He seemed to be better and I was happy. I thought maybe all we needed was some time apart to make the heart grow fond again and miss one another.

We still didn't have enough money to get an apartment, so I would sleep in the car with him in parking lots after the kids went to sleep at night. Of course, my cousin did not know this. I felt as though we were homeless with somewhere to stay, though I never told him I was feeling that way. (The sad part of sleeping in the car was that we still had our home back in Mobile.)

We eventually had enough money to get a hotel, and then an extended stay unit, which is like a tiny studio apartment. The boys would come stay with us as much as possible.

After months of that, we finally got our first apartment in Marietta, Georgia, and things were still going well. We were so happy to just be back together as a family under one roof. The boys were ecstatic to have their father with them as he spoiled them rotten. The house back in Mobile, Alabama was being rented to a relative. Paul was getting work every day. He had always had favor in getting jobs because he was a good worker with a great personality.

The prettiest smiles hide the deepest secrets. The prettiest eyes have cried the most tears and the kindest hearts have felt the most pain.
-Unknown

Everyone that talked to him just fell in love with him. The kids were doing well in school and we were making ends meet. I thought it was all over and we were getting back on track. Little did I know, what was about to come.

Here we go again.

It started with the small things. The arguments about nothing, the strange things that began to happen, things moving from where they would normally be, and on and on. "Here we go again!" I thought.

I was working full time and my clientele had picked up due to the prospecting that we did as a family. I would make flyers promoting myself selling fine jewelry. In the evenings and on my off days, we would take them to all the businesses in the surrounding areas. We always worked together for the betterment of our family.

If the fly on the wall could talk and tell of the hell we were starting to go through again inside our walls the story would seem very different. It was hard to go to work on a daily basis with a smile on my face like I was living the good life, when my reality was not knowing when the walls were going to come tumbling down on top of my head. I never really spoke about my family, especially not the problems we were having. I only talked about my husband as the man he used to be, never to put him down because of what we were dealing with, or what he was becoming. I threw myself into my work.

I remember one time Paul and I had gotten into it and again, for no reason at all, and I had gone through enough. I called the police and they asked him to leave for a couple of days. He ended up going back to Mobile.

One particular day weeks later, I had worked all day. When I came home from work, I needed to go to the store to get food and supplies for the week. Walmart was in walking distance, but not right around the corner. Any distance is too long when you have been on your feet all day long for 12 hours a day at work.

Anyway, the boys and I made our way to Walmart and completed our shopping. I remember praying on our way home that someone would offer us a ride. Mind you, I probably would not have taken it, and risk the boys' or my safety. It would have been nice to be asked, though. But GOD!! Right in the nick of time, who drove up looking for us? None other than Paul May, Sr.

I remember saying I serve a right-on-time God, don't we, because He knew I was on my last leg....last step!

Getting back to the story, pouring myself into my work was the only way I was able to handle it all. Normally, when you get off work, you return to a happy home. I would return home from work, just to be in misery. My husband would be very agitated and restless, walking the floor all night long drinking black coffee, which did not make his restlessness any better.

The kids did not know what was going on, or so I thought. One minute he could act like all was going well and the next, someone was messing with him some type of way. You can imagine their confusion, especially with him being the good father he had always been and the love they had for their father. He could not hold a job, even though he would always try to find another one just to lose it as well.

He started working when he was 17 and always took his jobs seriously. It was sad to see that he could not work and provide for his family as he had always done. I could only imagine how difficult that was for him because everything he was feeling was very real to him.

Time went on, and still, Paul could not find nor hold a job. He became very withdrawn at home, locking himself in our bedroom for most of the day, not communicating with anyone. My car had broken down by this time, so we were operating with one vehicle. He would take me to work and pick me up almost every day. On days he did not take me to work, I rode the city bus.

When Paul took me to work, I would be scared about what he would say to other employees or customers if he saw them in the parking lot. I never wanted him to come inside of the location where I worked. I was afraid for others to even speak to him because I did not know the response he would give. He would sometimes make hand gestures that I'm sure no one would have understood because I didn't understand them or know why he was doing them.

I was embarrassed that someone would know my husband was mentally ill, as if he brought it upon himself. Even though I was embarrassed, I pitied him as well, because I knew it wasn't his fault. The man I loved was not the man I saw before me anymore. The father of our sons was not the father that I saw before me anymore, and that was a painful thing for me to endure. I couldn't even imagine what our boys were feeling, because this was their father.

Paul would find churches to attend almost daily. Going to church is one of the ways the mentally ill will try to bargain with God or cope with what is going on. He was always a religious man, but he became obsessed with religion, as if he were asking God to heal him from this terrible disease even though he thought everything he was feeling was so real. He would send money orders to the churches that came on television. He would give to anyone that he saw needed anything, as if he was trying to buy back his sanity.

Paul was always a gentle-hearted person, the type to give the shirt off his back, but this was different. It was like with whatever normalcy he had left, he was trying to bargain with God to heal him.

As his illness got worse, he would still go to church every moment he could and read bibles all day, but he couldn't focus on it. His attention span was extremely short. He would go to church and sit in the back, but he could only stay there for 30 minutes to an hour. He would begin to read the Bible, but say God only wanted him to read one verse.

Paul was always getting on his knees praying and talking to God. He would not let anyone touch him. People would try to shake his hand and he would tell them that God didn't want him to let anyone touch him. He was never mean when he would say that to them. He would lean and kind of whisper it. I never interjected when he would say that; I would just look at the person and smile as though I wanted to melt away. Needless to say, I was very embarrassed.

CHAPTER 7

I never thought things would get as bad as they did. Paul began to call the police every time I said ANYTHING to him. He would call the police every day after I would get off work and several times a day on my off day. The police were so used to coming to our apartment that they would not take it seriously when they showed up. Several of the policemen would try to talk to him about getting help because they had seen this type of behavior before on different calls.

Though they had seen this type of behavior, the police are not trained how to deal with the situation properly. Paul wasn't a person who was breaking the law. He had never been in trouble with the law before. He was a person who needed help because he truly thought that he was right in what he was doing.

I remember one policeman actually gave him a direct order to go get some help or the next time they were called he would arrest him. I could tell that frightened Paul and I knew he would try to do something to keep from going to jail. He was raised as I was, to be totally scared to go to jail for anything.

Paul woke up the next morning, showered, got dressed, and went to Health Services. I remember the THREE PIECE BURGUNDY SUIT that he wore that morning in the heat of the summer. He was always a sharp dresser, but never dressed like he was on this morning, except for going to church on a Sunday. He understood that people could not see that he had a problem because they only looked on the outside.

He looked very handsome that morning even though he had begun to lose weight, but it didn't look bad on him. He was always thin-framed. He never gained more than 15 to 20 pounds since high school, and he really knew how to dress to make himself stand out.

He actually listened to that particular police officer and went to the Health Department. I was so happy that he was going, even though he wouldn't allow me to go with him. He came back that evening and said, "They sent me home and said nothing was wrong with me."

I was so angry! Oh my God, I could have blown a gasket because he was so good at being able to fool people into thinking nothing was wrong with him. At that point, I wasn't sure if he had even gone to the mental health department because he didn't have any paperwork to support that he had actually gone there.

Things escalated from that point. I ended up having to go to the sheriff's office and notify them to come and pick him up because of the things he was doing and I just wasn't comfortable with him being there without him getting some type of help so we could find out what was really going on.

They told me what day and time frame they would come and pick him up. I woke up that morning, got the kids off to school and I went off to work. I had discussed with one of my neighbors what was going to happen without giving her too much of my personal business, so that she could keep the kids until I got home for work. It was hard for me to do because I did not trust her. Our kids played together often, so she would find reasons to come over to the apartment when I wasn't home. She always wanted to come in and talk. I remember one time I allowed her to come in trying to be nice and she tried to rearrange my entire apartment. I didn't even know her like that.

She would always ask my kids about their dad and, being the protective sons that they are to both of us, they would tell me. Even they thought it was strange. She began coming over to look for her kids when I wasn't at home. The kids were never in my apartment, just as my kids were not in her apartment. I finally had to put an end to that and ask her not to come to my house when I wasn't home. She said she understood because all of the problems she had with her ex-husband....ummmm hmmmm.

I was glad we had stayed cordial to one another because I needed her that day. I did not want my sons to have to witness the situation if at all possible, so I had to open up to someone for assistance.

Can you imagine having to go to work and pretend everything is going well, and having to smile all day long and your heart is breaking into a million pieces at the same time? Hoping and praying your children are going to be okay because you have never left them with anyone before? Praying that they would be fine once they found out that their dad would not be home for a while? Thinking of the questions I would have to answer when we got home to explain why their dad was not there?

I was trying my best to hold back the tears by keeping busy. It was the only thing I could do.

They only kept Paul for 24 hours and then they released him to come home. No medicine or anything. I just didn't know what else to do. For a few days after his return back home, he would stay in the room and just not talk to me. He would talk to the boys and play with them for a few minutes every day.

It wasn't long though; things started all over again,

especially after he would talk to his family. One of his sisters had cancer and he would call to check on her, or the family would call to update him. The stress was really too much for him to handle along with everything else he was dealing with, but that was his sister and they definitely did not want to keep that from him. They were always such a close family.

The police calls were still going on until I couldn't take it anymore. By this time he had lost his oldest sister. Within 30 days, he received a call that he had also lost his twin sister. That had to be the hardest thing he had to deal with beside his mental condition. Sometimes, I think he had to go through the mental illness during that time in order to be able to handle the death of his twin sister. They were always so close. They both had similar personalities, always being the center of attention by being the class clowns everywhere they went.

I always thought it was strange when twins could say that they could feel what the other twin was feeling. I remember a thought early in our marriage; Paul would have times of the month that seemed like he was having PMS. I remember calling his sister to ask her was it that time of the month for her, and she said yes. It was weird, but he was feeling some of the things she was feeling. That's how close they were. I thank God for not letting him feel her pain as she was ending her time on this earth. It would have been too much to bear for him.

Paul and his family have always been very close, so I knew this was tearing him up. He wouldn't allow me to be there for him because he thought someone had done something to his sisters and that's why they died. I was hurting because he did not allow me to be there for him for his first sister's death.

CHAPTER 8

By the time his twin sister had passed, I had finally put in for a divorce. I did not get an attorney because money was limited, but I was determined to get out of that marriage because again, I felt like I was going to lose my mind. I had to research and learn what papers I needed to file for the divorce to ensure it was all done legally. The court date was set for the day his sister was to be buried.

No one knew or understood the pain I was going through. I had to call his sisters to come to Georgia to get him because at that point I had to decide again what was more important: Paul, our boys, or me and my sanity.

Our boys were older by this time; a few years had gone by. Though I had tried to hide things from them, they could see some of what was going on. How could they not, because we were all in a two-bedroom apartment at the time.

While Paul was in Mobile, his family had admitted him into the hospital for help, but not before he called my job to speak to one of my co-workers. He told her that I was trying to kill him and that I was practicing Voodoo on him. She had no idea what he was talking about or what was going on. Remember, I never discussed my personal life like that at work. She confided in one of my work friends about what Paul had said and she passed it on to me.

Something I always dreaded had happened. I was sure she would spread it all around the store, but I never heard a word from anyone. She never spoke of the conversation to me. She only asked if I was okay. I knew something was going to have to change at this point, love or not.

Luckily, Paul was already in Mobile with his family. They could see that something was wrong with their brother and his mother could see that something was wrong with her son. They were still upset with me because I decided to divorce him on the same day that his twin sister was being buried. No one cared about what the boys and I had actually gone through.

Before reaching the point of divorce, I tried several times to get him help here in Georgia. The laws are there to protect the mentally ill so that people can't just put them away. The problem is they are so protected that you can't get your loved ones any help—help that they greatly need. I tried repeatedly to go through the court system to have the sheriff come pick him up.

The law is the same now as it was then. Two people must stay in the household with the person and see that he is at risk of causing harm to himself or to others. They did not want to hear all of the crazy, abnormal things that he was doing. He had to try to hurt someone.

I told his family that I needed someone to come to stay with me and no one ever came, because they didn't think anything was wrong with him. Of course, no one was going through this but our boys and me. Why would others be concerned with what we were going through? They wouldn't, until it is put back on them. Then they saw, but still could not understand why I had to go through with the divorce.

He was in a hospital within a couple of weeks, so I guess they could not take it for as long as the boys and I had to endure his behavior. The only explanation I could give is that Paul was so good at holding a conversation when he contacted them, that they thought I was exaggerating the situation. Time had passed as I was still checking on him through one of his sisters. Everyone else in his family thought I had abandoned him and gone on with my life, which was far from the truth.

CHAPTER 9

Paul had gotten out of the hospital and of course, no one wanted him to come back to be with his family, but that is all he wanted to do. Nothing and no one could stop him from loving and wanting to be with his family. He would travel to Georgia on a regular basis to see his family, and even though I was scared that it would all happen again, I was very happy to see him each time.

At this point Paul was diagnosed with schizophrenia and bipolar disorder. Later in 2015, Paul was diagnosed with just schizoaffective disorder. The condition is so complicated that a misdiagnosis is common. Some people may be misdiagnosed as having schizophrenia. Others may be misdiagnosed as having bipolar disorder. Those diagnosed as having schizoaffective disorder may actually have schizophrenia with prominent mood symptoms.

It is so important to get more than one diagnosis for your family member. Mental health issues still need a lot of attention to help our loved ones adequately. Once he was released from the hospital he had to go to the mental health department monthly to ensure he was taking his medicine. I will talk more about this place later in the book.

While Paul was away in Mobile, I began to do research on mental illness. I didn't know anything about mental illness, so I had to start from scratch. I had so many questions. How did he get it? What did he do to get it? This is such a misconception! Was this going to be passed on to our sons? How was he diagnosed with both diseases? Was there a cure for it? If he took the medications, was that going to make him normal again?

The more I read, the more questions I would have. After putting a name to what he was going through, I was terrified about what our future would look like if I stayed with him.

One of the things I did find out through research, and something that I had never heard any doctor, nurse, or counselor tell me, is that patients often get off of their medications several times over the years because they feel better and normal again. This is something that the patient's family should be told.

Mental health professionals should properly educate us. It's not putting fear in us to tell us the whole truth. Trust me, we will find out one-way or the other. Why not tell us at the beginning of treatment, so that we know how to properly care for our family members. We are uneducated, thinking that once we have a diagnosis and the medication, that our family member is going to be okay.

Almost 75 percent of patients stop taking their medications because they do not think that they are sick. Another large percentage of patients stop taking the medications because of the medications' side effects. Most stop taking the medications when they begin to feel better. Though we may not understand this reasoning, it happens a lot. Most patients feel as though they do not need the medications anymore.

If I decided to stay with him, more than likely, I would have to go through him getting off his medications multiple times. I asked myself, "Do I want to put myself or my boys through that anymore?" I felt as though we had been through more than our share. It would have been easier for me to move on and find someone else. Actually, it would have been much easier emotionally and financially. Especially financially, because I was now the breadwinner, being blessed with the income I had, but having two good incomes would have been so much easier financially.

Did I want to weigh love against money? Love was the one thing and the only thing that kept me from doing just that. I loved this man like I loved myself.

The Mays

All I could think of was the man that was present before he became ill. I could still see the man that I fell in love with. The man that loved me so much. The man that loved his boys. The man that loved his family. All of the memories flooded my mind of how this man was when he was on his medications. I really couldn't think of another man really competing with him to share my heart with.

Love won every single time. Not just the love I had for him, but the love he had for me and his family as well. I think it's only fair to add that though my Paul was sick, he was still extremely handsome, sweet, well dressed, and adorable, which is part of the reason that, 99 percent of the time, no one knew he had an illness. He could have gotten another good woman, without a doubt. Women were always checking him out.

I truly believe he felt the same as I did. He only wanted to be with the boys and me because he loved us. He has never had self-esteem issues, so he knew he could get another woman—just not a woman to replace me.

Even through his sickness, Paul always remembered what he had said to me when we first met. I was different than most women, so there was no replacing me. BAM!!

To most people, Paul and I were both invisibly damaged. No one could see or tell what we had really gone through, not even his family. My mom would have been the only one who knew what was happening and had happened, because she was my mother, counselor, and prayer warrior. She was also Paul's best friend and advocate. No one could replace this jewel that she had found in her son-n-law.

CHAPTER 10

It was at this point, I had decided that I wanted to make Georgia home for my family and me. Paul was still in Mobile, coming back and forth to visit us often. I had begun to look for a home for us to purchase. I had talked to the Lord (as I always do before I made any major decisions in my life) and asked Him to allow us to purchase another home if we stayed in Georgia for five years. I stayed true to plan on our fifth year in Georgia.

Homes were much more expensive than in Alabama. I was shocked at the prices. I made good money by this time, so I could afford a nice home for us. I also had to remember I was the breadwinner, and alone. I still didn't know where Paul and I were headed. I knew I still truly loved him and I never thought about meeting anyone else. I didn't think I could ever stop being in love with Paul or loving another man the way that I loved him.

I am always true to myself and it was only fair to be true to anyone else that I would get involved with. Who wants to be with a woman when she is telling him she is still in love with her husband that has mental issues? No one.

Anyway, I did not want another man around my boys. I had seen too many of my friends and family members go through the stepparent drama. I never wanted my boys to have to deal with that. I loved them too much. So, if that meant I had to go through life without a man, so be it. My children were my life and so worth the sacrifice. Not saying it was easy, just saying it was worth it.

My sons would have made life unbearable for me and another man anyway. They loved their dad way too much. I remember how they would say that they were the only ones out of their group of friends that had both of their parents together. We could always see how important that was for them.

I remember a few instances where men would complement me and women would complement their dad and the boys would get so upset and give the men and women such nasty looks. They would come home and tell on whichever parent was getting the complement. They loved their parents and we loved them. They had already gone through so much already. Why put them through any more than what was necessary?

My mother came to Georgia to help me look for a house. We rode and rode for over a month together. I remember really wanting to purchase a home in the subdivision that we currently reside in, but none were available or all were under contract.

My mom saw a lady cleaning out her garage and told me to come back and check on that house because they were about to put it on the market. I asked, "How do you know that?" She said God had told her. She was such a woman of faith; it irritated me that normally, she was correct.

After a few months, I finally found a home that I wanted to purchase. What was the first thing that I did? I called Paul to ask him to come down to see the house to make sure it was the right purchase even though my mother had already checked out the house with me.

See, I have always had Paul with me any time I had made

any major decisions. We have been together since we were teens and our entire adult life. He had been a part of every decision made in my life. This one would be no different.

Probably in the back of my mind, I knew that this house would eventually become his home as well and I wanted his approval. I would have never told him that at the time, though, even if I thought it.

Of course, Paul was extremely happy that I reached out to him. He immediately came to Georgia. As he would tell you now, he always knew I would always take him back because of the love we shared. I tried not to follow my heart on so many occasions, failing with every attempt.

Meanwhile, I was waiting for our new home to close. It was I know everyone is wondering where Paul had been during this time. Yes, he stayed in Georgia with his family— with us. Needless to say, I wanted him here to assist me in the move, and I wanted him here because I wanted to be with him. He was doing so well and again, we were as happy as a family could be. The kids were so overjoyed to have their father at home once more..

Paul and I never looked at our relationship as being divorced. He still called me his wife and I still called him my husband.

I agreed that the only way we could stay together as a family was for him to have his medicine administered in injection form. By this time, I had researched more on controlling the disease to see if anything would work better than taking the medicines orally. I was not going to let him go through this illness alone; we would go through it as a family.

My prior research said that a person taking medication for this illness would often stop taking the medication, and that is exactly what Paul would do. He thought he was feeling better and didn't need it anymore, so he would just stop taking it all together. Then we would be back at square one going through the same problems. I wanted to find something that would assure me that the medication was getting into his system.

We always had to be so careful because there were so many side effects to each medication that also made patients not want to take the medication. Weight gain and sleepiness were the worst, especially for Paul because he has always been slim and always wanted to be a contributor to the family. Paul's appearance was always so important to him, as well as being able to do things around the house and for his family, even more so since he could not work. He always cared about how he looked in his boys' eyes, or anyone's, for that matter. He (and I) always went overboard doing things for our sons and telling them how much he loved them.

It was important to Paul that they knew how much he loved them no matter what his sickness was. It would sometimes anger the boys because they would feel as though he was treating them like little boys. He still does to this day, and they are both grown men, because he still wants them to always remember how important they are to him and how much he loves them.

I'm more like, "After 20-plus years of raising them, they should know by now." We were different in the ways we showed love to the boys and the ways we disciplined them, if you can call what he did "discipline." "Spoiled them rotten," is what I would call it.

Paul did not have a father growing up; Paul was only two years old when his father passed away. He always wanted to be there for his children and always wanted them to know he was there for them. The boys sometimes abused this to get their way to do things that I would not approve. They knew he would fight the battle with me on their behalf.

I knew all the tricks that the three of them had up their sleeves, though. Sometimes, I would let them think they were getting over on me. It was priceless and funny to see the love between father and sons. My prayer was that this bond would forever be between the three of them. I loved my boys and I loved their father. Seeing this bond between them made my heart smile.

CHAPTER 11

A couple of years went by with no problems. The injection was working perfectly with some side effects, of course. Our older son made a decision that we supported fully: he decided to go to high school in our hometown, Mobile, Alabama. He thought he would have a better opportunity of getting a scholarship in basketball at one of the high schools there.

The community that we moved into had just built a new middle and high school. Our son did not think the school or players would receive the recognition needed to get him a scholarship. He was completely correct—except he received a scholarship in football, as we will discuss later in the book.

Our older son went to stay with my mother. Paul was homesick anyway, missing his family, especially his mother as she was elderly with some illnesses of her own, so he decided to go back to Alabama to be with our oldest son. He said that Paul Jr. needed one of his parents in Alabama with him because it is so easy for boys to stray away and he definitely didn't want that to happen to either of his sons. I was to stay with Kendrick here in Georgia.

It was great for Paul to be in Alabama to help his mother out as she was getting older and could hardly get around. We would travel back and forth between Mobile and

Georgia to spend time with one another and as a family. It was hard, but as parents this is what we thought was best for our sons.

Kendrick truly missed his father during the time that he was away. Of course he would, because he was the baby and his father treated him as such. He was too proud to ever say it, but I could tell because I knew my son. My son used sports as he always did, to keep his focus off of his home problems. Basketball had always been his passion and focus.

We decided that Kendrick needed to go to private school to ensure we were setting him up for success in school and in life. Public school just did not understand him, the way he learned, or what he was going through. Maybe it was that they just didn't care.

He had a lot going on and it was hard for him to concentrate in school. They allowed him to come to before- and after-school tutoring, yet he still did not do well in their classes. He would just sit there and not ask any questions or for help.

I explained this to his teachers and shared what was going on in his home life, being very open and honest, thinking this would help them assist my son so he would not fall by the wayside. It did not. They allowed him to just sit there, and he didn't ask them any questions and they never asked him any questions. That showed me that the school or teachers really did not care whether he was successful or not.

As a parent, I definitely cared and wasn't going to let him slide through the cracks. I wasn't really thinking about him playing basketball; I was more focused on his academics.

Wouldn't you know it, the school we transferred him to was a great academic Christian school as well as champions on the basketball court. This pleased Kendrick. He was getting the academic assistance needed, yet still had the opportunity to play basketball as he so loved to do. Kendrick promised me that he would get a scholarship to help pay for his college tuition if we allowed him to play basketball for the school. I thought that by allowing him to continue to play basketball, he would concentrate more on his studies and it would continue to take his mind off of his problems at home.

This school was strict on academics, so he was required to go to tutoring before and after school to ensure his success. If he wasn't at early morning 6 a.m. tutoring, I would receive a call from the teacher asking if we were on our way. The basketball team traveled a lot and he was still required to do well in his studies or he would not be allowed to play basketball. I was happy with this policy because it made him focus more as well.

His basketball coach was unlike other coaches that he had been accustomed to. Kendrick has a strong personality, so he needed this type of coach at the time. They had a love-hate relationship the four years he attended the school. Some days Kendrick loved him and some days he absolutely hated his coach, who just happened to be the pastor of the church and assistant administrator of the school.

Paul May Jr's High School Graduation 2010

CHAPTER 12

Our oldest son graduated from high school, so it was time for Paul to come home, so I thought. It would be great having him home again because Kendrick and I both had missed him a lot.

I had gotten my real estate license while Paul was away. I was trying my hand at something else to bring more money in because I had seen so many real estate agents be successful in this market.

I remember saying I was going to be the top Realtor. I went into the office every day. I learned as much as I possibly could. At every opportunity, I would host open houses for other agents to get the practice in talking to potential clients. I would have clients say they were ready to purchase, so I would line up houses to show them.

No one had told me that I should have made sure they were preapproved for a loan, so I could locate homes within their means to show them. I also wasn't taught that before going out in the field to show them homes, I should have gotten them to sign an agreement stating that they would use me as their real estate agent when they found the home they wanted.

I used so much of my time and gas... I guess I should

use the correct word....I wasted so much of my time showing houses to clients who could not afford them. Some purchased houses from Realtors that were friends instead of from me, even though I found and showed them the house.

I had taken a leave of absence from my current job, using money from my 401(k) for a year to fully pursue real estate. I was putting in my all and getting nothing in return. No one was really teaching me what I needed to know even though I was with a real estate company. They saw my drive and aspiration. They had to. I was in the office daily trying to learn as much as possible because I didn't know how to half-do anything that I took on. Real estate was no different.

They were not even teaching me the basics. I had to remember, this is the world we live in. Everyone was out for themselves, not to help others.

So by the time Paul returned home, the real estate market was going down quickly. I went back to my prior job selling fine jewelry. Though the money was there, I wanted a challenge. I wanted to do something different so I only went back part time and was going to stick with real estate part-time.

CHAPTER 13

With the depression of the real estate market in 2008, people were deciding on how they were going to pay their bills and save their homes. No one was buying much jewelry anymore; that was a luxury that most could no longer afford. Even the customers I had that were well off were feeling the effects of the depression.

I had to search for another job. What else could I do? I remember riding home one day after work, the next day before work, and at lunch, thinking about what type of job I was going to apply for. I remember seeing people on their cell phones. In cars, at the bus stop, walking through the mall, even riding their bicycles. I decided then that I was going to work for a cell phone company because it didn't seem like the depression was affecting this part of the business world. I began to complete applications to wireless companies that night when I got off of work.

I finally landed a job with a communications company here in Georgia, not knowing anything about the communication business. I was still carrying around a Razor flip phone when everyone else was using a smartphone. I did know that people where purchasing cell phones and using them. That was a great start for me because they definitely weren't buying much fine jewelry anymore.

Here I go, having to learn something all over again.

In the meantime, while Paul was supposed to be ready to come home, our oldest decided that he would work that summer before college. My son's so-called friends had wrecked his car, so he did not have a way to get to work. The travel was about an hour each way to work. So Paul, being the father that he was, decided to stay in Alabama to take him and his other co-workers to and from work daily until he could find a way to get to work.

This went on for a month or more until our son and a couple of his cousins decided to rent out an apartment together by the month until college started.

The sacrifices we have made for our children to ensure their safety and success in life.... I guess that's just what we do as parents. Every last one of them was worth it and I am not complaining.

CHAPTER 14

Paul finally came home and all was well again. I had missed one of the most important things I think really helped us stay so close to one another: the power of touch.

I often ask couples if they are in love. The response most times is that they really love one another. Loving your spouse and being in love with your spouse are totally different. I think we get so caught up with the woes of life, we forget that no matter what is going on in our lives, we must continue to touch one another in a gently loving way.

I missed lying in bed and having Paul just rub my body down with his fingertips, just caressing me for hours... caressing me as we lay on the sofa watching television. This has nothing to do with making love, but it is a part of intimacy. To be transparent, we would normally end up making love that night.

Love-making has always been so important to us both because it connected us to one another. I remember while Paul was on one of the medications, our love-making slowed down to only four times a week. I made him a doctor's appointment to see what was going on.

The doctors asked us what our normal routine was and I said seven days a week, sometimes twice a day. He said,

"And what is it like now that it has you worried?" I answered four times a week.

He looked at me and said, "You know I'm younger than you both and my wife and I don't make love that often."

My response was, "AND? What do we need to do to get OUR normalcy back?"

The power of touch and love-making is so important to being in love. I really can't stress this enough. Try it. Do your own test. Do not touch or make love for a couple of weeks. You will notice that you and your spouse will not be at ease with one another. Then try making love for two straight weeks or as often as you can and enjoy. You will see how much your feelings have increased for one another. The power of touch and love-making is one of the most important actions for your relationship, right there with communication and trust. Okay, off of my soap box and back on subject... Lol

CHAPTER 15

Of course Kendrick was enjoying the attention of both of his parents. Kendrick played basketball year-round for multiple basketball teams. He had us traveling all over Georgia and other states with him. He always knew how to get his way with his dad, being the baby boy and using his dad's absence as leverage. He was getting any and everything he wanted.

School was in again for Kendrick, so we got him together first and then off to get our oldest ready for his first year of college—an exciting time for any young man.

We moved him into his dorm as a family. The excitement of being on your own was in the air. We were proud parents and brother, talking about the expectations of Paul, Jr.'s freshman year in college.

We were on track for a while. Kendrick was in school, Paul, Jr. in college, and me on my not-so new job learning a lot, and already having my eye on a promotion. We only had one car, so Paul would take Kendrick to school first since he had to be there early for tutoring and basketball practice. Then, he would come back and take me to work. Luckily, we lived, went to school, and worked in close proximity.

Paul would return in the evening, pick up Kendrick first from basketball practice, take him home, and then pick me up from work. We needed another car, but with a son in a private college and a son in a private high school, it was extremely expensive. On the other hand, I did not know how long Paul was going to stay on his medications, and I needed to keep the bills where I could take care of everything without his contributions to the household. It was not easy, but it was what we had to do in order to make it all work for the betterment of our family.

Paul felt he needed to do all of the driving around, as if the shoe was on the other foot. I was thinking that if it had been me, I would have been pissed off on a daily basis. To my surprise, when the roles were swapped, we adapted well. I became the breadwinner and he became "the stay-at-home dad and husband."

Still bringing in income, Paul was proud to be contributing to the household finances. He took being a stay-at-home husband and dad just as seriously as he did any of his other jobs. He enjoyed taking care of the yard and house including preparing dinner in-between playing taxi for our younger son and me.

Kendrick would routinely forget his lunch so that he could have his dad purchase him lunch from a fast food restaurant. He knew that is something I would have never done. Kendrick was spoiled to say the least, but was very good at pretending that he wasn't.

CHAPTER 16

A couple of years went by and we were doing great as a family. As I had stated before, there are side effects to the injections. Paul had a doctor's appointment, but I wasn't able to take off work or change my schedule this particular time.

I remember receiving a call while at work. It was Paul. His doctor at the time wanted to speak with me. She wanted to tell me that it was time for Paul to stop the injections because of the side effects they were causing.

I remember being so angry because I knew he was not going to take the medications like he should. I tried to tell her that, but she said if he did not stop taking the injections his side effects would be permanent. His mouth had started to tremble Involuntarily.

I knew it was for the best, but I was just thinking about the past, and all of the research that said those with this illness would stop taking the meds when they thought they were better.

My worst fear didn't take too long to show its ugly head – it happened within six months. It began with little things happening. We were getting into arguments and not understanding why we had to keep going through this. Just thinking to myself, "If I can just get him back on his meds we would be happy again. We can be the perfect family because when he was on his meds that's what we were."

Remember I said he would do everything for us because he was trying to make up for not working anymore. Our roles had changed. I was the breadwinner and he took care of home, and when I say he took pride in everything, he did.

He took care of his responsibilities better than I could have ever done. He would cook and have dinner ready for us when we got home. He would fix my plate and bring it upstairs as I showered and prepared for bed. It was absolutely perfect and it took a lot of the stress off of me.

I truly needed that because I had begun to put myself in place to be promoted. With the manager I had, he really made it hard for me to be promoted. It seemed as though he was working against me in every way, so I really had to fight for my leadership to be taken seriously.

I was dealing with so much. I was having trouble on the job, as well as having trouble at home, all while trying to make sure we raised two strong, healthy, and productive young men to send out into society.

I felt like my sanity was slipping away. What was to be done? What could I do to save myself? No one at work knew what I was going through. I was always preaching that you couldn't bring your problems to work. I definitely couldn't bring my problems to work. I was not able to confide in anyone because I knew that if my manager found out, he would definitely use this against me. He tried to use anything he could to keep me from being recognized and promoted.

Finally I was recognized for the work that I was doing and in line to be promoted. I was excited and scared at the same time. I had so much going on personally. I loved my husband, but I also loved my work and helping others. I had to take this next step at this time in my career. If this promotion were not taken, there would be no telling if or when it would come around again with the manager I had because he was not trying to get me promoted. I really felt like he was trying to hold me back.

Thank God someone else saw my potential. I was going for it, no matter what else I had going on. This was my chance. It would also bring in more money for the family as well.

I had enough on me by this time and it came to that point again where I had to decide what I was going to do concerning Paul. Luckily, I had the support of his family this time, and I needed their support.

CHAPTER 17

Paul and his siblings have always been very close. His next to the youngest sister had a little more pull with him than the other siblings. Not because she didn't spoil him, as they all spoiled their baby brother, but because she had no patience when it came to foolishness, taking control, and doing what was necessary.

I knew him and his actions so well by now that I knew if I could get him to her in the next week or so, she could scare him into taking his medications again. It was a small window of time, so I needed to hurry. I had to tell him that his mother and sister needed him to come back home to help take care of his mother. His sister and mother had to agree to do this with me.

This was the only way he would leave. I don't care how bad he got; he never wanted to leave the boys or me. He would tell me how much he loved us and how much we needed one another. It's like he would be sane just enough to at least remember the good in his life for that moment. No matter how bad he got, he never missed a night calling us to say he loved us. Even when he was back home and I wouldn't answer the phone because it was just too hard to talk to him in that condition, he would leave a message to let us know how much he loved us. That was strange in itself because he hated talking to the answering machine, even in his best times. He always hated answering machines.

As we had projected, his sister threatening to have him committed to get him to take his medications worked like a charm. Even though he was back on his medications, he decided to stay with his mother for a few months because his sister truly needed the help with their mother. He loved his mother and wanted to help take care of her. I was good with that because I knew how much he loved his mother. She was getting older and sicker, so he needed to spend time with her because no one knows the day nor hour that will be our last day here on this earth.

CHAPTER 18

Paul became lonesome and missing his family, so he returned home. Yes, we were missing him just as much and very happy to have him back with us. I was catching a ride to and from work, which wasn't the easiest thing to do. Kendrick was riding with another child that lived a mile or so away, which worked out perfectly. The parent was happy to help without taking any gas money for her troubles. We were blessed that her son not only went to the same school, but played on the same basketball team as well.

We were very blessed when it came to getting others' assistance in taking care of Kendrick when I was at work. It was like God planted us in the exact neighborhood and house. I have never been a trusting mother with my boys, but one of my neighbors really earned my trust. She was like a second mother to my son. I knew every day where he would be if not at home. If he wasn't over there, she would question her son as to where he was because she knew I was at work. We carpooled to take the boys to their practices, games, and outings.

Most of the burden fell on her because I worked so much. My son or I never heard her complain. I am forever appreciative of her for ensuring my son was safe and still continued to stay active even though I wasn't able to take him all the time. I am forever in her debt.

Thank God things were so good for the next few years again, leading up to our youngest son's graduation.

Kendrick May High School
Graduation 2013

CHAPTER 19

We both were so proud of Kendrick. He received a scholarship to play basketball paying for his college career. He kept his promise to us. He said, "If you send me to private school, I will receive a scholarship to help pay for college." Paul was so proud of his boys and loved them so much. He knew they had been through a lot. He knew he had missed out on being there sometimes when they needed him the most. Though it was out of his control, he still battled with missing out.

I'm sure the boys still battled with that as well, if the truth would be told. Our young men, like most young men, rarely show emotions and you definitely couldn't get them to talk about it. Mainly, I would do the talking, trying to provoke conversation about it in the hope that they were listening. I just wanted to know that they were all right, but how could they be all right? It was hard on us all, including Paul.

"My May Men"

CHAPTER 20

It seemed life was moving along just fine. I had gotten another promotion and loved it. Reminiscing about my tenure at this company, I remember calling my boss and telling her that I needed to step down because my husband was sick and I needed to devote more time to him without telling her too much.

I told Paul about my decision when I got home and he was furious with me. He made me promise to call her and to tell her that I was not going to step down. He promised that he would do better. He said that he could not live with himself knowing that I wasn't going to be able to do what I loved to do and it was because of him. He reminded me of how hard I had worked to get to where I was in my career. I did exactly as I had promised him because, truth be told, I never wanted to step down. I felt that it was my obligation.

My mother had just returned home. It was such a great visit though she did have some medical issues right before she left. Her specialist here in Georgia had to reset her heart rate because it was irregular. This was the only procedure that she had ever allowed him to do except for running tests. Jesus was her doctor, and though she followed the doctors' orders in taking the medications, she would pray for an answer before she would allow the doctors to do any type of procedure.

Jump-starting her heart seemed to work because I could see she had more energy. She was always so feisty and spicy. I didn't like seeing her not being as active as she had always been.

As I worked more hours, there were more conference calls, more people to influence, and I was really enjoying my new role at work. Then came the day that changed my life forever. December 17, 2013. I was involved in a critical car accident, causing a severe head concussion. My lungs were damaged, both bones were completely broken in my right leg, my knee was busted up, I suffered two blood clots, and pneumonia.

I had an awful stay at the worst hospital in the world. I had never been sick before myself, but in visiting my mother, family, and friends during their hospital stays, I have never, ever been in a HOT hospital before. As I said, both bones were completely broken in my right leg. I had an external fixture on my leg and thigh to keep my leg together, and my leg was quadrupled in size because of swelling. I had to wait for the swelling to go down before surgery could be scheduled. After a surgeon visit, my insurance company tried to send me home to wait.

The hospital and I fought with the insurance company, but it seemed we had lost. I was being discharged and had no idea how I was going to even get in a car to get home. My husband was on his way to get me and his plan was to take me to a hospital that was closer to home because where I had the wreck was three hours away from our home. He didn't care what the insurance company said.

By the grace of God, as soon as my husband arrived, we received the news that I was being transferred to a closer hospital. This transfer saved my life. I was transported to the other hospital in an ambulance, which was very painful and uncomfortable.

Now can you imagine being transferred back home in

the back seat of a car? Lord, the pain would have killed me.

Immediately after arriving at the new hospital, I knew that the care was going to be so much better. The coolness of the hospital was the first difference that I noticed. Then it was the professionalism and care of the staff. I had the best care possible.

As I have always had long hair, I felt that it was crawling with germs from not being taken care of properly at the other hospital. No one ever offered to wash it. Can you imagine sweating a week in the hospital and not getting your hair washed?

I'm so glad I was removed from that other hospital. I have no problem in saying that I would have died from my leg or something getting infected because of the lack of care I received.

The first thing I asked for from the first nurse that entered my room was a pair of scissors. They looked at my husband as if I had lost my mind. She brought the scissors into the room and I cut every strand of my hair off, to the skin of my head.

Everyone thought this was being drastic, but I did not want to bring those germs into this new hospital, giving them time to get into my cuts and scrapes. Hair does grow back, but I couldn't grow another leg back. It was an easy choice for me.

They also are the ones who found out that I had the blood clots and pneumonia because they listened to my complaint. They started therapy immediately even before I could have the surgery. I am here today because of the care of my team of doctors (my Surgeon Dr. Garrett and Pain Management team Dr. Alan and Dr. Paul), nurses, and physical therapist Teresa. They not only took care of me physically, but mentally as well. They motivated me, ensuring I never gave up.

We didn't tell my parents until I made it to the second hospital. My mother had just gone home the month before, trying to keep her strength up, and I didn't want to worry her until I knew more about my condition.

She and one of my aunts arranged to come to Georgia to see about me, with the assistance of my cousins meeting at the halfway mark between Georgia and Alabama.

A mother has to put her eyes on her child when illness strikes no matter the age. For my mom, being an evangelist, she had to lay hands on her child and pray for her child. Those prayers have gotten me through some pretty tough struggles.

They stayed a week, and I so needed them there. One of my cousins, who is like my sister, was there for me as well. She came to the hospital nearly every day to help as much as possible. I just really needed the company. I also needed someone to adjust the temperature controls for me. Though I was too hot at the first hospital, I was extremely cold at the other.

We found out that my iron count was low – so much so that I had to receive a few pints of blood to get my count to normal. That is one of the reasons that I stayed so cold. It would really get lonely in the hospital, even with constant company. The walls of the hospital would feel as though they were closing in on me even though with all of the pain medications they had me on, I should have been asleep most of the time.

I wanted to know everything that was going on, so I fought sleep as much as I could. Really, who can sleep in a hospital with the nurses and other hospital personnel coming in and out, doing what was necessary to make sure you were recovering well?

Other family members, friends, co-workers, and mentees would call and visit often as well, which was very nice. It's always nice to know that others care about you. It was already extra hard having to spend Christmas and New Year's in the hospital.

Paul was there with me every single day for almost two months. The staff was so in awe of him because the only thing they had to do for me was give me my meds and therapy (and he was there for that, as they allowed him).

He would bathe me every morning and every night and get me dressed, change my linens daily, change my diaper, put me on the bed pan, get my dinner prepared once he arrived, wash my hair daily, be my voice to the doctors and nurses, anything I needed. He did it all because he felt like he knew how particular I am, so he didn't want them rushing me to do anything. He would have patience with me, allowing me to assist in turning myself.

Some things he already knew how to do and others I would teach him. In one of my previous jobs I was a Certified Nurse Assistant, so I would teach him how to properly take care of me! He was so eager to take care of me. He always felt as though I was so strong that I didn't need him to take care of me. Little did he know, I have always needed him in spite of my strength.

That is such a misconception about strong independent women. Being strong and independent does not mean that we do not need or depend on our men. As you have read throughout this book, I needed Paul as much as he needed me. I felt as if I wasn't whole without him, although I was complete. Could I function without him? Yes, because I am a strong woman, but I am stronger with him because I have him to lift me up when I am weak. When I am down, I need him to help lift me up. When I am unmotivated, I depend on him to motivate and inspire me. To remind me of the woman I am. He did this so often for me.

Though I am a strong woman, I need my strong man to stand with me. See, you have to be a strong man in order to understand and deal with a strong woman. To know how to say things to her that would make her submissive rather making her feel like she's being docile. We are so opposite in our demeanor, in how we handle situations, even in the seasons we like the most. He may not even tell me that he dislikes something that I did, but because we knew one another so well, I would automatically know that he did not approve of it.

A strong man knows how to handle a strong woman.

With all of what we had gone through, I thank God for my strong man. I needed him more than he would ever know. Maybe not in the ways he wanted me to need him, but in my own way. I think he really enjoyed taking care of me during the most vulnerable time in my life.

I remember two sayings that my parents would say to me about us. My mother would say that I better not ever leave Paul because no one else would ever put up with me or spoil me as Paul does. My dad would say that Paul treats me like he did fishing. He would let me run the line so far and then he would reel me back in. I was glad to know that they knew how much Paul loved their daughter.

CHAPTER 21

Further along in my hospital stay, both my mother and mother-in-law became ill. My husband, being the son he was, wanted so badly to be there for his mother and for my mother, who was his best friend. He was torn because he wanted to take care of all of his special ladies.

His mother made the decision for him and told him his place was at my side, which relieved him, but of course, he was worried about our mothers. This was so hard for me being the only daughter and having only one brother who was sick himself.

My brother was shot in his heart on December 24, 1995, walking with a relative to that person's house. He was robbed at gunpoint on church grounds. Thank God a friend of the family saw the incident along with our cousin and came to my brother's rescue. Our friend threw him in his truck, rushed him to the hospital a few miles away, and came to alert the family of what he had witnessed.

What a Christmas that was for our family. It was touch and go with him dying on the operating table three times. This is the testament to the faith that my mom had in God. Each time the doctor would come in the waiting room and tell her that her son was not going to make it, she would say, "NO! God is not ready for him yet."

Each time they would go back in and do a little more.

Her son, my brother, survived that bullet shot to the heart. He was a testament to what God can do even in the mist, when it looked like the end many times over. You can choose to believe man's word or our Creator's word. She chose God's word and her son lived, was alive and well.

My mother had been sick for years, but I had always been there for her when she was sick, even when I worked or when I was a child. I had been there for every procedure, whether inpatient or outpatient care. I was always there for her before I moved away. I was always able to stay in the hospital with her or go to doctor visits, so I would know what was going on.

When I moved to Georgia, I still was very active in her care, or as active as she would allow, being the spicy woman she was. Though her sisters and my cousins assured me that they were going to take very good care of her, I wanted so badly to be there by her side. Even as I was in the hospital trying to recover and piece my life back together after the wreck, I would have her call me when the doctors came in her room so that I could speak to them and find out first-hand what was going on with her condition.

Paul and I would pray together every day for their speedy recovery. At that point that's all we could really do, along with checking on them both daily to let them and family know that we were concerned.

As I was ready to leave the hospital, it was bittersweet because I realized that it was really time for the healing process to begin. I still could not walk on my right leg, but with further home therapy I could learn how to do things for myself again and regain the use of my leg. Though I was on some very strong medications, I was still in a great deal of pain. I had to sleep in a hospital bed downstairs because I could not walk up the 13 stairs in our home.

CHAPTER 22

I had a doctor's appointment a week or so after being released from the hospital. I remember hearing that we were going to have some type of snowstorm in Georgia, but it really didn't click as to how bad they were saying the snowstorm was going to be. I really didn't want to miss a doctor's appointment, so we went.

It looked like any other day outside. Snow was nowhere in sight. I asked Paul to stop and fill the car with gas. Normally, he would only put $20 to $30 in at a time. This time he did as I had asked.

We got ready to leave the doctor's office and snow began to come down very heavily and very quickly. We had to travel over an hour to get back home. Eighteen-wheelers were pulled on the side of the road, they were sliding down the hills, and cars were just sliding everywhere. We made it about 30 minutes from the house on the snowy Interstate 285 to get to Interstate 75 South. We get there and cannot make another move. Cars were sliding and accidents were everywhere.

Our oldest son was coming from work and he had gotten stuck in the snow as well. His dad was so nervous. He felt so helpless that he could not get me home and now he could not get to his son to assist him. We knew we were going to be in the car overnight. There was no way of getting around any of the cars on the interstate. We were too far away to try to get to any hotels or convenience stores.

Luckily, for the first time, Paul had done as I had asked him to do—to fill the car with gas. At least we would not freeze to death. The cigarette lighter did not work in Paul's car so we could not charge up our cell phones. After a couple of hours we lost contact with our son.

I thought Paul was going to try to walk to where his son was. Now, we were nowhere near him, but Paul was so worried that something would happen to Paul Jr.

The worst part of the entire ordeal is that I had forgotten my pain pills. I had already gone through withdrawals a few days after I was released from the hospital because no pharmacy had the pain medications in stock. I remember I was screaming, yelling, praying, and feeling like I was going to lose my mind; I had no idea what was going on. Twenty-four hours of that was enough.

I also remember the following morning seeing my older son look at me helplessly as he ran downstairs after hearing my screams. Paul said, "You are okay. Let's pray about it." I said, "Yes, let's pray as we are on our way to the ER." I knew something was not right and I needed them to fix me. I thought I was losing my mind. Withdrawal was the diagnosis.

So now trapped in the snow, I began to go through withdrawal again after several hours had passed. You cannot be on strong meds and not take them for hours. Drugs are no joke. I was screaming and shaking in the car again, with Paul trying to console me the best he could.

I could not walk, my leg had just started to heal from all of the surgeries, and I did not have pain medication. Prayer was my friend in the time of need if ever I was in need.

By morning, Paul decided that he could maneuver around the other cars because they had been sliding and shifting throughout the night as others were trying to inch forward. He was always such a great driver and truck driver. Lord, I was so scared that we were going to get into a wreck or killed. Our tires were not the best on the car and I was sure they were not snow tires or all-weather tires.

Paul made his way around those cars like we were in an arcade game. He kept saying, "Hold on baby, I'm going to get you home safely." We only slid one time the entire ride home.

My hero got me home safely. I was smiling and blushing. My man, MY HERO!! The best part of it all was when we got into our neighborhood, on our street, and close enough where we could see our house. We saw our older son's car in the yard.

Paul began yelling and praising God. He was so happy that Paul Jr. made it home safely. Paul Jr. had Googled several times using different techniques to get his car unstuck. The search told him to take out his rugs and place them behind his tires to provide some friction. It worked and he made it home warm and safely. Paul hugged him so hard. He saw that we had raised our boy to be a man to think for himself. It was a proud daddy-son moment. We were all safe and sound.

I learned from this adventure. Never leave the house when you hear there's a snowstorm coming and never, ever leave the house without my pain medications!

CHAPTER 23

Home therapy lasted for a few weeks, then I began outpatient therapy, which was my second blessing. I had the best therapist and one of the best therapist assistants that anyone could ever ask for.

The personality of my therapist assistant made me want to come to therapy and work as hard as I could. We would talk about everything, taking my mind off of therapy, which was making me work even harder.

I remember our first conversation. I had been trying to ride the cycle, but I could never get the paddle to go all the way around. I realized that after talking to her for about 15 minutes, I was rotating the paddle all the way around without even noticing the pain or that I was going all the way around. She was awesome.

I remember when she was transferred to another facility, I was so sad. She was just the therapy I needed for my mind. They were all good for my body, but she put my mind in a better place. I was progressing along well, though I would be in therapy for years.

Paul always made sure I did my follow up exercises at home and though he wanted to do everything for me, he made sure I would do as much for myself as possible. He knew how important it was for me to become less dependent on him.

Paul invited my three preteen cousins (we already had our 2 1/2year old little cousin staying with us) to come to Georgia to spend the summer with us. He had me going somewhere everyday on the days I did not have therapy. We had season tickets to White Water and Six Flags for everyone. We were at one place or the other. If we were not there, we were bowling or doing some type of craft show.

He never gave me a chance to get depressed or to give up. I could only take a few steps at that time so we would rent the electric wheelchair for me to get around the parks or he would push me in my wheelchair until I was able to take more steps using my walker. He was such good therapy for my mind until I stopped paying attention to where his mind was leading him. He was so attentive to me until he stopped being attentive to his needs. He was sacrificing himself for my recovery and me.

I was so wrapped up in trying to get my life back together that I didn't see Paul's life was beginning to unravel again. The pressure was so much on him having all three of his favorite women sick. Both of our mothers were now hospitalized.

I began to notice little things, but not often because most of the time I was so medicated on pain meds I could barely remember the things I needed to do. He was only taking half of his medication because he was trying to have more energy to take care of me. One of the side effects to his medication is tiredness and sleepiness with loss of energy.

I would fuss at him to try to get him to take his meds in full but to no avail. He still took very good care of me, doing everything I could possibly need him to do. I had a sitter that would come for six hours a day for a few months, but Paul did most of everything, even though I could see the effects of not taking his medications starting to show.

He would leave when the sitter would come and no one knew at the time where he was going. He would say, "I was just riding." That was not good because we didn't know what else he was doing. By this time, my mother was getting worse and I knew I had to get there to see what was really going on.

I wasn't ready for what was about to happen.

I had to call my doctor to get permission to travel. I remember it took them too long to get back to me and by the time they did, I was already on the road headed to see about my mother.

I was blessed to have my dad to help check on her as well. They had been divorced for over 20 years and he remarried during that time for 10 years. Even so, he and my mother remained very close, as they had begun dating at 11 and 16 years of age, respectively. Yes, she was very fast in her younger days.

Though others were checking on her and making sure she was cared for, it was time for me to come and see about my mother myself, no matter how much pain I had to endure. I was blessed to travel in my condition, but I really didn't have a choice.

I remember when we arrived and I rolled in her hospital room in my wheelchair, she said, "I told my sisters that you were coming today."

I asked her how she knew because I hadn't told anyone. Of course her response was that the Lord told her.

The Lord gave me two days to spend with my mother before He called her home. The night before she left us, she was transferred into ICU because they could not get a blood pressure reading or find a pulse. She was as alert as any normal person. She was giving me instructions about what to make sure I removed from this room to take to the other room or home. Their attitude was, you have more important things to worry about. She continued giving her instructions as she often did with her spicy little self.

I remember getting up to take my shower so I could head to the hospital. While I was in the shower, I could hear a voice as plain as day say that it was time. I remember this voice because I had heard it before, years ago; back in 1997, when I thought that my mother was going to have to be put on the heart and lung transplant list.

I remember driving and praying to the Lord not to take her yet, because I wanted her grandsons to know her and all of her values that she would teach them. This was the same voice I was hearing again in the shower saying, "It's time."

I answered back saying, "I am ready." I got out of the shower and was getting dressed to head to the hospital when I received the call that she had passed.

I really didn't understand what the doctor had told me the night before, or I was in denial. They told me that her organs had begun to shut down. After asking several questions that she wanted clarification about what the doctor was saying, she decided that she wanted to be classified as "DO NOT RESUSCITATE." I agreed because we both had talked about that years ago. That should have been my reality, but it wasn't.

I thought somehow it was going to be weeks, or even months.

Ms. Joann C. Powe - My Mother

When I arrived at the hospital, she was lying in bed like she was just asleep. She looked just as beautiful as an angel. She was now my angel.

Remember, during this time Paul was not taking his full medications. He was taking a half of a pill. So, Paul being in his condition, he could not stand to see her without life. I could not get him to come into the hospital with me.

He and my mother had always been so close since we started dating. They talked daily; even if I didn't talk to her on a given day, which would have been rare, I knew she was okay because her son-in-law would have spoken to her. I was so thankful for the bond between them.

He was becoming more withdrawn as we prepared for the funeral. No one could tell that he was off his medications but me, or at least no one let on that he was acting strange. If they did notice, they probably just said he was grieving heavily.

Remember, most people that we knew did not know Paul was going through a mental episode. Even some family members did not know about his mental illness. He was so good at hiding his symptoms from others. He was still doing everything I needed him to do, but he would disappear back to the hotel room until I called or needed him. I was surrounded by family and he knew if he stayed more than a few minutes that someone would be able to see that something was wrong with him.

I have always been amazed by that ability. The fact that he was having a schizophrenic episode, he was able to think of how to not show it to others or be aware that others could tell.

My Mom and Paul - Best Friends

CHAPTER 24

A couple of weeks after the funeral, we returned home to Georgia. Paul's episodes were about the same though he was withdrawn from the family. I was still in recovery mode and trying to keep my senses together after losing my best friend, my mother. Paul began to always have somewhere to go, which is the next phase. Once he hit that phase, there is no talking him into getting back on his medications.

Months had gone by and things were just getting worse. My blood pressure was rising and the nurse could not figure out why for the first week or so. Paul would often talk to the nurse outside before he entered the house when he would make his home visits. I never told my nurse what I was dealing with, but after a week or so, he realized that something was wrong with Paul, and told me I needed to get him some help for us both.

I had to once again call on my sister-in-law for assistance. Though she agreed to have him to come back to Alabama under the pretense of taking care of his mother again, she really needed the assistance because their mother was getting worse. She had become bedridden at this point after experiencing three strokes.

I think because of the stress she was under, Paul's sister didn't pay his symptoms any attention for a while. She worked full-time, was a foster mother, and took care of her elderly bedridden mother. She was glad to get the help. Months had gone by and as time progressed, Paul went into the next phase, where he was still capable of functioning on a daily basis, but thought everyone was against him. He wouldn't eat any food that someone else cooked; he thought everyone everywhere he went was trying to do something to him. He was still helping to take care of his mother at this time.

Another month or so went by and he was getting worse. He was eventually in a car wreck. Yes, he was still driving. He totaled his car in the wreck. Came home and didn't say anything to anyone about the wreck. We found out when the insurance company called his sister as they were on the insurance together. I was told he would park the car so that the wrecked part could not be seen.

The insurance company totaled the car out thankfully because Paul did not need to be driving at this time anyway. For the first time since he was 17, Paul did not have a car. He began walking to where he had to go after his sister went to work and his mother went to therapy. They began getting reports saying that he was seen in certain areas acting unlike himself. Remember, we are from a small town where it seems that everyone knows everyone or someone you know.

Finally, his sister had to have him taken to the hospital against his will for his safety and so we could get him better again.

I had to make the trip to Mobile a couple of times to make sure he was getting the treatment that was needed. I wanted to make sure he got a second option on his diagnosis. We needed to be certain he was on the correct medication, and to find out if that medication came in injection form.

I was already dealing with my husband being hospitalized for a mental illness and all that it encompasses. Up late one night thinking about everything that was going on, I received a phone call that my brother had been in a fatal car accident.

I had just returned to Mobile to see Paul, to make sure he was in good hands, and let him know that I still loved him. I knew that I would be there for him no matter what. He had proven to me time and time again that he would always be there for me. I knew once we got him better, he would return home. Only this time, I made it mandatory that he be put back on the injection. I knew that was the only way we could have a chance to make more positive memories to overcome all we had already gone through.

Though the doctors did not want to put him on the injection, his sister and I continued to push back and demand he be put on the injection.

Paul with my brother, Darnell O'Shea Powe, during his last Christmas with us!

CHAPTER 25

So I had to head back home to help my father bury his only son, my only sibling, my brother. It was only the two of us, my brother and me. We were like twins being only 11 months apart. I helped to take care of him when our mother passed and he was helping to take care of our father. He was killed in a hit-and-run car accident.

I think his death hit me harder than my mother's because it was so unexpected. I felt that my mother had lived 62 years and had been sick for a long time, still pushing forward. He was only 44 years old. I still felt as though he still had his life in front of him. It was also how violent the wreck was, leaving his body in the middle of the street for other cars to run over. Because it was raining so hard that night, it was a possibility that they could not see him lying in the road. I wouldn't have done a dog like that, let alone a human being.

It was even harder because I did not know whether my brother called out for me and I wasn't there for him. We didn't know at the time whether he had died on impact or not, until one day the person who found him lying in the road sent me a direct Facebook message. He told me that my brother was alive in his arms when he stopped and found him in the road. My brother did not speak to him, but he was breathing and he did have a heartbeat. If the person who hit him had stopped or called 911, who knows; maybe he would have made it.

From the report, we know now that due to the extent of the force with which the car hit my brother's head, he would not have made it.

My brother's death was like losing a child to me. I was the older sister who always took care of her younger brother. Our parents worked a lot when we were in grade school, leaving me in charge of making sure he did his chores, homework, and was kept safe until they returned from work. I remember I would do his chores so that he could go to baseball and football practice. I remember when we were in middle school, I would fight anyone who would try to fight my brother. I was my brother's keeper. Now he was gone. Now my mother was gone. My father and I were the only ones that were left here to continue to live on without them.

I had no idea how I was going to do that. I was still grieving for my mother. Before his death, my brother was *really* grieving our mother's passing. He was the baby and lived around the corner from our mother, so he was able to see her on a daily basis. It was extremely hard on him when he no longer saw her during visits with his neighborhood friends.

I always calmed myself with the thought of my brother's spirit looking up and seeing his mother, his angel with her hand extended outward, saying come on home my son. I can see him smiling from ear to ear with excitement, seeing his mother again. They are both my angels now.

My brother was not a person to harbor hard feelings. If he saw the person again who ran him over and killed him, he would give him a gentle kiss on the cheek and say, "I know you didn't mean to do it."

That is just the type of person he was. He would irritate me often, but I could not stay mad with him for long. He would call me every single day to say, "I love you," and I would always say, "I love you too, brother."

I am so glad I have that precious memory to get me

through the difficult times when I am down at my lowest. I don't have to assume how my brother felt about me because we told one another often.

Paul's sister and I both agreed that we were not going to tell him about my brother's death right away because he was responding to treatment so very well. I knew that he would demand to be let out to be with me if he found out. Paul's sister and I thought it was better this way.

I knew I had to tell him before the funeral. He was in the perfect place to get help dealing with the grieving process once we told him. We had told the doctors and nurses about the grieving he still needed to do for my mother because he wasn't taking his medication during her passing. He and my brother were very close. My brother would call Paul to take him to the store or where ever he needed to go when Paul was in town. I knew there was no way I could let him miss his funeral.

Before we had the opportunity to tell him, he found out while one of my brother's neighbors was at the hospital visiting her grandson. She had told her grandson of my brother's violent death in a hit-and- run accident.

He and his roommate were having breakfast the next morning. Just in general conversation, his roommate mentioned what his grandmother told him. Paul asked what the guy's name was who got killed because we both grew up around the same area where my brother lived and was killed. He said my brother's name and my husband asked him again to say the name. He then asked him did he have a nickname and the guy said the name they called my brother.

Of course he was beside himself. He immediately called me, blaming himself because he felt as though if he hadn't been in the hospital, he would have called him to take him to the store and therefore would not have been killed in the accident. I had to explain that he had no possible way of knowing that and in no way, shape, or form was he responsible for my brother's death.

We are Christians and believe once your date is written in the Book of Life, you will leave on that day. His date was written and had come to pass. It was his time whether we were ready for him to depart this earth or not, just as it was our mother's time. We had to accept this fate and the only person to blame was the person that hit my brother and did not stop to call for emergency help.

Paul was ready to get out immediately. I pleaded with him to give his sister and me an opportunity to talk to the doctor to see what he thought we should do. I still needed to make sure he was on the injections and responding well to them. I also wanted to make sure he received grief counseling while he was already in the hospital. So, we needed to tell the doctors all he had been through in the last two years with my wreck, my mother's passing, his mother being bedridden, and my brother's death.

He stayed in a few more days for counseling. He was so happy to be able to be there for me, but so sad to lose my brother. I was happy to have the person that has always been there for me and by my side through everything I had ever been through since I was 16. I was happy to have the love of my life by my side, as it should be.

Yet another tragedy in the books.

CHAPTER 26

We returned home after a few weeks and all was great. Paul was on the injection, looking and doing very well. It was such an exciting time for us because through all of this we were expecting our first grands. Yes, I said grands. TWIN BOYS! So, it was extremely important that we get Paul on track and stable, not just for a little while, but for good this time. I became much more involved in his treatment. No one was going to take his joy away.

Paul was the proudest grandfather ever when our grandsons arrived. He has been a loving granddad as he has always been a loving father to our own two sons. The injection has worked and he continues on his treatment.

As we were enjoying not having to worry if he is going to get off of his meds, we began to notice that my father wasn't as active as he had always been. He was 69 years of age, so we just thought that old age was catching up with him. My uncle began to tell me that he would not show up when they had made plans to go fishing or to play golf. My father has always loved to do both in his spare time, but since his retirement that's all he would do.

I would question my father as we talked - as often as he would answer his cell phone. He would always say he was just tired, or it was too hot outside, or some other excuse so that I would not worry or continue to ask him questions. He has always been a light talker and likes to be left alone to do what he wants to do. Getting older, he was even worse at it.

I thought he was going into depression. My father had lost my mother the previous year. Though they had been divorced 20 years, they remained very close. He even stayed with her to assist in taking care of her when I could not get there because of my condition after the wreck. He had lost his only son who was helping to see about him after my mom passed, so he would see his son daily. He lost his niece to cancer within 30 days after my brother's death. He lost his youngest sister to breast cancer that following November.

Mr. Albert Powe - My Father

That had to be hard on anyone no matter how strong the person may be. It seemed as we were losing someone every few months. I guess when you come from a large family, you have to expect more deaths. The difference was that most of the family members we were losing were not the older ones; they were younger family members that you just didn't expect or weren't ready to say goodbye to. I had to remind myself of Job 1:21. He said, "Naked I came from my mother's womb, and naked I shall return there. The Lord gave and the Lord has taken away. Blessed be the name of the Lord." It helped to trust and believe in God, remembering my Christian training. That is the only thing that has pulled me through all I have endured in this life thus far.

We used the twins, his great-grandsons, to get my father to come for a visit for the holidays. They were born June 2015 and I had been sending my father tons of pictures getting him excited about seeing the twins.

David Paul May and Daniel Paul May

He was such a good grandfather to his grandsons and would love them 'til death. He loved teaching them how to fish, play golf, basketball, football, and baseball. He really enjoyed the conversations they had as they were growing up. I remember how proud my father was of them. Though he didn't believe in really spoiling a child, they knew that they could ask him for anything and he would give or get it for them. Most of all, he loved passing on his passion of golf and fishing to his grandsons.

My father had never been a big talker (even to me), and I know he loves me and has always been a great father to me, but he could talk to those grand boys all day long. I knew sending those pictures would make him want to play with those great-grands. Not only did he agree to come to visit us for the Christmas holiday, he really wanted to hold, touch, and kiss those great-grand boys that for months he had only seen pictures of— their plump, beautiful, smiling faces with eyes so big they were like flashlights at night.

Daddy's Girl Always!

Now that he was in Georgia with us, I could see that his energy was very low and his feet and ankles were swollen often. We talked about going to the ER. Of course he refused and said he was fine. He never liked going to doctors at all which is common for most men, and especially for men that lived alone with no one pushing or making them go.

I had to call in the big guns. I had to call his older sister to persuade him to go to the ER. After a conversation with her, he agreed. We got him there quickly, before he had time to change his mind. Within the hour, the doctor comes into his room in the emergency room with a statement I could not believe.

All I could think of was that I was about to lose my entire family within two years. GOD, WHAT'S GOING ON? I was always taught not to question God, but that's all I knew to say at this moment. I felt like I was being punished for something. I know we all sin and come short of His glory, but I did not think I had done enough to deserve all of these deaths right together.

I remember my husband reminding me how strong I was and telling me I was going to be just fine. He said the words I was so tired of hearing these last two years, but knew to be true. "THAT GOD DOESN'T PUT MORE ON YOU THAN YOU CAN HANDLE."

I said God must definitely know something that I do not know because I am in the weakest state that I could ever be in. I was always so close with my mom, but I was a true daddy's girl. Just remembering in the flash of a moment how he had ALWAYS been there for me in my childhood and even more as an adult. If I called him and said I needed anything, he made a way to get it to me that day. Never complaining. Never even asking me what it was for. All he knew was his little girl was in need and he was still my hero that was going to take care of me.

My hero was at his weakest state at this point. This

could not be happening.

The doctor came in and announced that we had two choices and we needed to decide quickly. Either he had emergency dialysis right now or we needed to start the HOSPICE process. His kidneys had almost completely shut down. His sugar was extremely high. He had a leaky valve in his heart. His thyroid was too low. His blood count and iron were extremely low. You name it, it was happening to my father.

He was in his right mind, so he made the decision.

I was busy crying because I was just like, O.M.G. is this really happening right now?

He decided to have the dialysis. At this point, we knew he would be moving in with us after over a month in the hospital. He started outpatient dialysis. He was on eight medications including one for his diabetes. After the first round of dialysis, his blood sugar dropped under 20 and he was going into a diabetic coma, which I thought at first glance that he was having a stroke.

Paul and I had stopped at Home Depot for about 10 minutes after we picked my dad up from dialysis. Thank God it wasn't any longer. He told us that he was thirsty, so Paul bought him a PowerAde back to the truck to drink. We get to the truck and my father is almost non-responsive. My husband asked him what's wrong. He mumbled that he was cold. I looked in the truck at him and pushed my husband to the side and said, "We have to get him to the ER now!" We arrived at the emergency room to find out that his sugar had dropped below 20. They stabilized him, released him and we went home.

They educated me of some things to do incase this happened again including calling 911 instead of trying to drive him to the emergency room. Sometimes the adrenaline takes over and you go into panic mood and just do what needs to be done. I remember driving so fast blinking the emergency lights and blowing my horn so cars would let me by. Running red lights to get him to the hospital in time. My concern was mainly for him.

We were only about 10 to 15 minutes from the hospital, but it seemed like it took us an hour or more to get him there. I remember my husband jumping out at the emergency room to get a wheelchair and I had jumped out and grabbed my little daddy out trying to carry him into the emergency room. As much pain as I was in I couldn't feel a thing at that time. He was my main concern. He only weighed about 138 pounds at 5'6", but I felt it when that adrenaline rush went away. I now understand how real it is when people actually pick up cars and we are all amused at how they could do that. Adrenaline will have you doing the impossible.

The next morning my husband asked my dad what he wanted for breakfast and my dad wanted pancakes. My husband goes to get the pancakes and makes it back within 10 minutes. When he came back to give my dad his breakfast, my dad was non-responsive yet again. His sugar was below 20 - again. We call 911 and began to give him chocolate frosting as they told me to do the previous day in the emergency room. The reason they said this is because it would melt on his tongue, bringing up his sugar level as we wait for the paramedics to arrive.

What they had not told me was the mess that we were going to make. We had chocolate everywhere all over his clothes and mine by the time the paramedics arrived. They didn't know what had happened, but it did bring up his sugar level, which was the desired result.

He then had to be taken to the hospital, but not before I told them that I definitely had to change his clothes. There was no way possible he was headed out this house looking like he had pooped everywhere. Not on my watch.

They had gotten my dad's blood sugar above 60 by the

time I had quickly changed his clothes. They rushed him to the hospital after explaining the same thing had happened the day before. He was admitted and we stayed there another month. His body was not dissolving the diabetic medication which was why the sugar level was dropping so low. My husband had been my rock and by my side through all of this. We both stayed in the hospital room with my dad 24/7 to make sure he was taken care of properly. Paul's injections have been the best thing ever for Paul and for us.

We got my father stable. Dialysis was (and still is) working well for him. But Paul's mother's health had started to decline during this time. We received a call that she had to have surgery and wasn't doing too well. We had to get him home to be by her side. I could no longer just pick up and leave. My father's dialysis had to be scheduled in another state a month or so before because he could not miss a treatment.

Of course, we talked several times a day throughout the time she was in the hospital.

Ms. Lou Ella May - Paul's Mother

Paul and His "Hero"

CHAPTER 27

I so wanted to be there for him as he was always there for me. God decided to give us another angel. This was the testing point for Paul. Paul has always been a momma's boy. I just knew this would destroy him. He had a hard time, but by the grace of God he was coping very well. He was trying to be strong for his family and for us, but I could see how devastated he was.

Losing your mother is all-together on another level. The saying goes that no one will love you like your mother. That unconditional love felt from your mother even when she is scolding you.

Paul's injections are working and we are thanking God. He is enjoying life, his family, and especially his grandsons. He helps daily with my father, ensuring he is well taken care of even though I do most because I know it is my responsibility and I want him to know that I want to take care of him because I love him.

This is the heart of the man I fell in love with so many years ago. Though we have had our share of troubles, trials, and tribulations, he has always loved me. He has always loved his boys. I have never had to question or doubt that. He loves his brothers, sisters, nieces, and nephews. He is just a loving man that doesn't like confrontation unless you mess with one of his boys. Then you will see the other side of his personality that rarely comes out.

Though we have been through a lot, I would not change a thing because it has made me the woman I am today: A woman of strength with a man who loves her. I have never blamed him for this disease and I know and understand it is not his fault. I will not blame him or allow him to blame himself for the tragedies we have been through. It is no one's fault. No one is to blame. God had a plan. He knew the plan. He allowed us to come through all of it with a love so strong that it is unbreakable.

The Mays – Whole and Complete

CHAPTER 28

I have cried so many tears. I have questioned the Lord and asked, "Why us Lord", but I never ever stop trying to get Paul help. I will never ever stop loving him. I wanted to and couldn't. I tried to and couldn't. That's how I know God gave us to one another. He placed love so deep in our hearts that a mental illness and all that comes with it could not break us. I will never EVER give up on him. He has shown me a type of love that most women will never get a chance to see. Mental illness or not, I love this man until the day that I die.

It is so important for us to share with our family members what is carried in our DNA. We cannot afford to be so proud, scared, and secretive about what is going on within our family. I know going back in time that's how our elder family members were. Sometimes even sharing more real stories of our family instead of just saying they are drug addicts or alcoholics. Remember, some of the actions that they were displaying before that. A lot of time alcoholism and drug abuse is a cover for a mental illness that has not been diagnosed.

We need to know who had high blood pressure, cancer, heart disease, diabetes, and so on. When you have a medical problem, your treating doctor always wants to know your medical history. He wants to know if there's something in your past that may affect your current condition or your treatment plan. He needs to know if there's any family history of similar problems as well as what medications you are on.

Knowing your family's medical history is important because the treating doctor needs to know this information not just for the sake of writing this information down on a form, but because it can sometimes alter the different possibilities you might be suffering from as well as their treatment plan for you. Sometimes there is not a reason why we get different diseases. Sometimes you may be the first to experience that disease in your family, but more often than not, this will not be the case. We must break the silence and talk about what we are sharing with our family. It could open up so many doors to the treatment that will help make us a healthier family. Please share with your family and break the silence.

My Hero – Paul May, Sr.

Paul has always felt bad because he could not give me the material things that he could not afford to give me. He plays the lotto as much as he possibly can because he wants to bless me with the house, the jewelry, and the car he thinks I deserve.

Not ever trying to say that the struggle was easy, not knowing how we were going to make the ends meet, or knowing how we were going to just do what we needed to do for the family and a few things that we wanted to do – no, it wasn't easy. But I am truly happy with what God has blessed us with. We could have any big beautiful house, but the love that we have as a family makes this little lovely house a true home. I would not want to ever change that and risk not knowing love of family as I do now. This love that we have was kissed by God's lips and he made it perfect just for us.

The Mays in Love

Loving and Leaning On One Another

So Blessed!

The Mays on the Red Carpet in Atlanta

What I want others to get out of this book is to know that there is love after a mental illness diagnosis. You can have a fulfilled life. You can still love your spouse through the struggles, and there will be many. I need you to remember this. You must recognize the signs, you must be willing when no one else is willing to get your loved one some assistance, you must become active with their doctor visits and medications, and you must stay strong.

The important thing that I want to share with you is never ever give up if the love is worth the fighting for. Thank God I never did or I would have missed out on this beautiful love that Paul and I share. You can have this too.

I would not change anything for this journey.

A Love Kissed by God's Own Lips!

Following is an insert taken from a letter that Paul wrote me while I was away in basic training going into the Air Force

Dear Kal,

I hope you are doing fine up there. I am not doing to good down here because you are not here with me. Three months is a long time to me and I know it is a long time to you too, but Kal I am not going too late you down because I love you. It's hard for me down here. Kal buy when I think about me and you is going to get married when you get back, it makes me stronger and happy. The reason I was not home on March 24, 1989 on Friday is I was not in the streets. I was getting the curl in my hair. Kal I really miss making love to your fine self. I am going to wait for you and when you get back we are going to get a home and you are going to be my wife because I love you and we want something in life. I want things to go right for me and you. I know I do not tell you how much I love you often. I don't know why I do that, whet when you get back I am going to tell you I love you every day. If you was in my heart you will know I much I love you Kal. So Kal that's all I know to say.

Kal I hope you are not getting upset up there. I hope you do what you got to do so you can come home to me. I miss you so much. I hope you know that and I love you. Kal do not be mad at me for not writing you. You know I am not a good writer. Kal I believe in you and I hope you believe in me. I love you. I hope you be my wife, my loving wife when you come home. I know we will be happy. I know I will when you come home to me. I love you. Do not forget, I love you because if you know that I love you, you will stop worrying about home and me and do what you got to do and come home to me. Believe in me. Know I love you. Please know I love you and just do your work so you can come home and be my wife.

Your loving husband,

Paul A. May

An insert of a letter from my mother pleading for her future son-in-law

Let me tell you something. If you and Paul are to be married, you have to stop listing to everyone else. They will break you and Paul up because they don't want you to marry him because they are jealous of y'all relationship. You have to trust him if you are going to marry him. You got him worried to death thinking that when you get home you are not going to marry him. Your friends are about to run Paul crazy calling behind him trying to see what his is doing and where he is every minute. Tell them to stop call his home worrying him. You already know how much Paul loves you and what he will do. Paul, your daddy, and I went to church together Sunday. He is so sad and misses you so much. I think he really loves you. If he don't he might be fooling me, but stay on thinking for yourself and never be foolish for anyone. Love you very much and hurry home.

From your mother,

Joann C. Powe

Our eldest son gave me the perfect Mother's day card that describes how he sees me as his mother through all the struggles we have overcome.

I don't know where our family would be without your TENDERNESS, STRENGTH, and LOVE.

You do so much to make us all feel happy, cared for, and supported. You're our heart, our rock, the center of our world.......

Happy Mother's Day

ABOUT THE AUTHOR

Kayl May is an Author, Radio Talk Show Host, and Successful Customer Service and Life Coach. This U.S. Air Force veteran enjoys inspiring others to use their gifts and abilities to improve the world around them.

Kayl has plenty of experience finding the good in a world full of challenge. Her husband, the love of her life, battles mental illness; she lost her mother and brother within a few months of one another; and she survived a near-fatal car accident that left her leg severely damaged. Yet through it all, Kayl has built a successful life. She and her husband raised two outstanding young men who blessed them with two grandsons. Her exceptional careers in fine jewelry sales and customer service led to establishing her own business as a corporate trainer on customer service and retention skills. And Kayl's decades long love of her husband Paul and their battle with schizophrenia led to significant advocacy work on behalf of the mentally ill.

To learn more about Kayl and to bring her into your organization, visit her website at http://kaylmay.wixsite.com/the-bottom-line/author.

www.ingramcontent.com/pod-product-compliance
Lightning Source LLC
Chambersburg PA
CBHW031148160426

43193CB00008B/291